T0110550

Also by James A. Houck, Jr., Ph.D.

The Apostle Peter: His Words Should Be Red Too

Redeeming the Bereaved: A Spiritual Model For Healing Woundedness

*Reclaiming Authenticity: A Psycho-Spiritual Process
of Transformation and Transcendence*

WHEN ANCESTORS
WEEP

*Healing the Soul from
Intergenerational Trauma*

JAMES A. HOUCK, JR., Ph.D.

abbott press

All Scripture quotations, unless otherwise indicated, are taken from the Holy Bible, New International Version®, NIV®. Copyright ©1973, 1978, 1984, 2011 by Biblica, Inc.™ Used by permission of Zondervan. All rights reserved worldwide. www.zondervan.com The "NIV" and "New International Version" are trademarks registered in the United States Patent and Trademark Office by Biblica, Inc.

Abbott Press books may be ordered through booksellers or by contacting:

Abbott Press
1663 Liberty Drive
Bloomington, IN 47403
www.abbottpress.com
Phone: 1 (866) 697-5310

Because of the dynamic nature of the Internet, any web addresses or links contained in this book may have changed since publication and may no longer be valid. The views expressed in this work are solely those of the author and do not necessarily reflect the views of the publisher, and the publisher hereby disclaims any responsibility for them.

Any people depicted in stock imagery provided by Getty Images are models, and such images are being used for illustrative purposes only. Certain stock imagery © Getty Images.

ISBN: 978-1-4582-2213-8 (sc)
ISBN: 978-1-4582-2212-1 (e)

Library of Congress Control Number: 2018912527

Print information available on the last page.

Abbott Press rev. date: 11/05/2018

DEDICATION

For all of humanity to embrace the value, dignity and worth of those
who have come before us,
those who live with us in the here and now,
and those who will follow us.
So that the people may live!

CONTENTS

INTRODUCTION

This book follows a basic premise in that throughout history, traumatic events have wounded and immobilized people. Not just in life-threatening or physical ways, but also in psychological, emotional, and indeed, our understanding of who we are as souls. Whenever, and wherever, there have been violent crimes committed against humanity, people are often overcome by horrific physical, emotional, psychological, and spiritual suffering. As a result, their assumptions about themselves, others and even God, have been shattered and their internal coping mechanisms have failed. Due to the severity of the trauma, humanity's painful memories, intense feelings, obscure perceptions, interrupted cognitive functions, and maladaptive behaviors, become encapsulated in time. For lack of a better word, people often describe themselves as being *stuck*, unable to move past traumatic events as they replay them continuously in their mind, body and soul. This feeling of being trapped in linear time can extend to days, months, years, decades and even centuries, as past, present and future generations often bear the scars of *once upon a time*. Despite the fact that our understanding of the subtle mind, body, and spiritual nuances of trauma has made leaps and bounds over the past several decades, the phenomenon of psychological, emotional, physical and spiritual encapsulation still occurs today. Moreover, although there has been much research done in how, when, where, and why people hold their emotional, cognitive, physical and spiritual trauma, precious little has been researched in how trauma truly affects the soul. Perhaps this is due in part to the limitations of western theological and philosophical debates that struggle to define what the soul is? In fact, there appears to be a great deficit in our language regarding how our minds and bodies express the soul, let alone, what to do with it now once we realize we are one? For example, most of the time, people are content to relegate the soul to something we give a nod to during religious services. We live our lives, go to work or school, plan our careers, form relationships, procreate, avoid pain, and engage in pleasure, without much thought of the soul...until the day we are faced with our mortality. It is then, perhaps, we passively rely on the soul to do its job and carry us into the next life. Rarely do we consider how to live our lives as souls, let alone treat one another accordingly.

As a counseling educator, mental health and pastoral professional, I have seen firsthand how trauma encapsulates the soul of wounded people. This insight was not something I was taught in seminary, nor did I learn this in graduate school. In fact, if the soul ever came up in conversation, it was always done so in the third person, often referring to the soul as *it*. This description is simply not accurate. The soul is not something we have, but instead, the soul is who we are; the purest essence of ourselves that is related to God. Every external sense about ourselves is simply *ego window-dressing*. Still, in my work with people struggling to make sense of their losses, grief, trauma, after-death communication encounters and near-death experiences, many find it problematic to grasp the belief that souls often become bound to the place where traumatic events have resulted in horrific, physical deaths. Just ask anyone who believes in *haunted* houses, battlefields, lighthouses, hotels, restaurants and boarding schools. These places often attract thrill seekers and ghost enthusiasts, seeking to confirm tales of sightings of *disembodied spirits* lurking about, but do nothing to transform the traumatic energy that has ensnared these souls, so they can be released from that place and find peace with God.

On the mental and physical level, traumatized people often describe themselves in the aftermath of tragedies and horrors, as feeling disconnected from not only themselves and others (*depersonalization*), but also feeling disconnected from their surroundings (*derealization*). In fact, if the intensity of the trauma persists and results in the death of the body, the more likely the soul will also experience a disconnection, and thus cry out to be reconnected to the *Soul of the Universe*, i.e., God. Ironically, this phenomenon has been the one aspect history has always underestimated about the voice of the human soul. For example, humanity has always attempted to silence people, societies and/or nations through orchestrated killings, murders, genocide, starvations, forced assimilations, humiliations, and degradations, often defining people as savages or primitive, backward, unworthy, unlovable, and therefore, disposable. Nevertheless, this phenomenon is not true for everyone. For the majority of people who experience trauma, they can emotionally, physically, and psychologically process their pain, find their soul's voice, and heal from the past. Yet, even when traumatic events result in physical deaths, the soul still can be heard. This is because we are energy in the purest sense, and therefore, our souls have a distinct voice of their own. Not even the death of the body can silence the soul because if there is one prominent lesson that comes from the field of physics, besides *gravity* and *inertia*, it is that energy can never be destroyed; it can only be transformed, and therein lies humanity's healing.

Throughout my own experiences, research and interviews with people from various cultures, I have learned that traumatic energy is not only passed down *intergenerationally*, but also traumatic energy has the potential to encapsulate the souls of both individuals and entire communities. Ironically, this communal encapsulation often occurs because the initial traumatic energy is reinforced through the rigid social systems in which we live: educational, governmental, religious, health care, community norms, environmental, judicial, correctional, etc. In fact, unresolved trauma is not the only phenomenon that has been passed down through the generations. Learned behaviors that encourage negative assumptions, prejudices, feelings of contempt and corruption toward a group of people, have galvanized these systems for centuries. These, too, have also been passed down from generation to generation to generation.

Nevertheless, the time has come to not only discover our own soul's voice, but also hear the cries of our ancestors; generations whose souls long to be healed from their trauma and released to God. Their stories are not over just because they are no longer physically with us. Indeed, they have much to teach us not just in terms of how they suffered and died, but rather how they lived and loved. Ellen R. White of the *Snuneymuxw First Nation* in Canada believes that unless we have a deep communication with our ancestors, much deeper than merely acknowledging our shared DNA, we will forever struggle to get below the surface in all relationships (Archibald, 2008). Therefore, the question we must ask ourselves today is: Can we enter our own soul in stillness and listen to their wisdom?

CHAPTER ONE

Blood That Cries Out:
Intergenerational Trauma

"What have you done? The voice of your brother's blood is
crying out to me from the ground.... Genesis 4:10

It all started with a drop of blood. I was visiting my Native American Indian elder, friend and teacher who noticed that I cut myself on his wooden chair. In all seriousness, it was a deep splinter from a rough board, but in the end, it turned into a life-changing lesson. Before I could wipe away the blood from my finger, my teacher grabbed my hand and told me to take a long look at my blood. He then asked me, *"What do you see when you look at your blood?"* *"I don't know what you mean?"*, I replied. *"Look more closely at your blood. What do you see?"* Again, I replied superficially, *"O-Positive?"* His tone softened as he looked directly at me. *"Look again at your finger, your blood. Who do you see?"* Ah! I was beginning to understand, but still struggled to put into words what he meant? We sat there in silence for what seemed to be an eternity. Finally, he broke the silence as he explained, *"There is life is your blood. Not just your life but also the lives of your ancestors and relations; generations and generations whose DNA and yours are all there in a single drop of blood."* I listened to his words, but they didn't exactly sink in. So, like many of my moments of profound insight, the most lasting lessons often begin during times of confusion and pain. Just ask me someday about the scar on my left thumb. Ironically, I of course, had to get below the surface of my bloody finger and perceive something that I had not been taught, trained or ever told to consider. *My relations? Generations? Ancestors? Just by looking at a single drop of blood?* My mind quickly took me back to my high school days when, as students, we looked at blood under a microscope in Biology class. Yet, since I did not typically carry a microscope with me, I had to rely on my teacher's years of skilled perception of the soul. *"Look again at your blood, and tell me who do you see?"* Thinking I understood what he meant I replied, *"I see my parents, grandparents, great grandparents and great, great grandparents."* *"Is that all?"* he asked, pushing me further. *"Yes"*, I replied as I further explained that this was as far as I knew about my genealogy. He curled his lip and raised his one eyebrow. From his expression, I knew I was not fully grasping his lesson. *"Do you not see all of the generations of those who have come before you, in whose blood, your blood, carries the DNA of their lives and yours? More than just every characteristic of genes, can you also see their personalities, character strengths, flaws, struggles, fears, triumphs, joys, and mistakes? Can you see their souls when they took their very first breath? Can you see them before what we call 'time'; that instant when the Creator dreamt them... and even you?"* My head was spinning as in that moment I felt like I was in a dream-state. Sensing I could handle more of this revelation, my teacher added, *"Once you can see those who have come before you, you will also be able to see those who will come after you; those who are alive but are yet to be born. You are all there in that single drop of blood."* Since that day, I never looked at a bloody finger the same again.

Most people I know do not like the sight of blood. From its unpleasing odor to its many associations with violence, many people have a phobia of blood. I myself am not even fond of having my blood drawn for tests. Nonetheless, I know without blood, we would not exist, and life would not continue. In fact, people who need transfusions know this all too well in that blood contains everything we need to sustain life: Blood contains white cells to fight off infections, red cells that carry oxygen throughout our body, and platelets that clot our blood when we bleed. In a sense, our blood is a liquid blueprint that carries our DNA, identifying who we are, the present status of our health, and yes, even the genealogy of our ancestors. Blood can tell us many things.

Ironically, despite these life-giving qualities, blood does have shelf life. In fact, Red Cross donations are typically kept no longer than five-six weeks. After this time, red blood cell membranes lose their flexibility and the quality of blood begins to breakdown. Furthermore, once blood is spilled, it leaves what appears to be an everlasting stain on our clothes, skin and pollutes the environment. Moreover, blood is probably the most stubborn of all stains to remove. Even after a thorough scrubbing there are still ways to detect blood stains on all kinds of surfaces, especially on the surface of our soul. Try as we may to scrub and sanitize every inch of contamination, we eventually realize that when it comes to our soul, it takes a lot more than cleanser and bleach to bring us inner tranquility. For example, at the trial of Jesus, the Roman Governor Pilate made a public display of innocence as he washed his hands of Jesus' blood, yet was troubled in his soul by his decision to execute Jesus (Matthew 27:24-26). Despite her obsessed scrubbing, Shakespeare's Lady Macbeth's blood guilt could not be removed from her soul, let alone, her hands (Macbeth, Act 5, Scene 1). Also, in Shakespeare's *Hamlet*, the story begins with guards anxiously reporting seeing a ghostly figure. We come to discover later in the story that the ghost is the King of Denmark (also witnessed by Hamlet), who reveals that he is unable to find peace and rest because he was secretly murdered. As Hamlet discovered more about the truth of his father's death, the more his mother became tormented by her guilt. In these and many more examples, the effects of one's violent actions lie not so much in the stubborn removal of blood stained crevices of hands and fingers, but rather the effects lies in the crevices of the human soul for both victim and offender.

Since the beginning of time, humanity has always tried to *wash their hands* from all kinds of atrocities and injustices that have been inflicted on the land and each other. Ironically, such crimes against humanity quite often seem to escalate especially when they are done for, and in the name, of God (Haught, 2002). In this sense, humanity is very creative in coming up with justifications for shedding another's blood, innocent or otherwise. If you have ever watched the Disney movie *Pirates of the Caribbean: Curse of the Black Pearl* (2003), you might recognize the phrase, *"Dead men tell no tales!"* as uttered by Mr. Cotton's parrot. Many people believe this was a phrase invented by pirates as the *swash-buckled* their way through perilous voyages in search of buried treasure. Even today hearing this phrase might make the hairs on the back of our neck stand up. However, neither Disney, nor the pirates, invented this expression. Instead, its origins can be traced back to a proverb by English Reformer Thomas Becon (1560), *"the dead cannot reveal any secrets."* Although this saying has existed for a long time, it did not gain popularity until it became famous through the Pirates of the Caribbean ride at Disneyland. Basically, to tell no tales means to keep something quiet, kill anyone who knows about it, and, since that person is dead, it would be pretty much impossible for him or her to tell your secret. A similar saying is *"three can keep a secret if two are dead,"* which was coined by Benjamin Franklin (1706–1790). Today, forensic psychologists, coroners, crime scene investigators and detectives investigating murder scenes, rely on the deceased to tell them all kinds of secrets as to who, what, when, where and even perhaps why, they died or were killed?

Interestingly, the westernized world of mental health therapy, medicine, spirituality and theology, must also discover the benefit of knowing how the dead continue to speak through the living. Perhaps despite what we have been taught in biology, theology or psychology classes, various personal experiences reveal that the dead do speak in many ways. In fact, they speak to us in our dreams, through our conditioned behaviors, attitudes, perceptions, thought processes, learned helplessness, work ethics, inter-personal relationships, phobias, addictions, etc., all handed down to us from one generation after another. Perhaps you may even know someone in your family who has a certain mannerism that is the spitting image of a deceased relative, whom he/she has never met. My grandmother always used to tell me that I reminded her of my deceased grandfather, who died in the coal mines when my father was two years old. She used to say, *whenever you sit and hold your head a certain way, you remind me of*

George! Even when I laughed I reminded my grandmother of him. As a boy, I did not know what she meant, but for her, it was as if George continues to live on in the family. Indeed, he does.

Family secrets and personal stories of injustices that were intended to be *taken to the grave*, also live on in present generations. In fact, those so-called family and society secrets are often revealed again and again and again through unhealed traumas that have been passed down through the language of blood, and the voice of the soul. In fact, for all our feeble attempts at sanitizing human history, blood spilled in the name of murder, genocide, Manifest Destiny, cover ups, the Doctrine of Discovery, slavery, forced starvation and encampments, lynching, and exterminations, to name a few, are still evident in both the land that holds the energy where blood was shed, as well as the souls that remain ensnared there. As stated earlier, these phenomena are especially true when such violent crimes against humanity were committed in the name of God. This fundamental belief used to justify such mistreatment of humanity is what Kevin Annett (2006), founder of the *International Tribunal into Crimes of Church and State*, describes as: *that when God is on our side, we can commit any crime; we are absolved individually from that crime by believing we have a higher sanction... and that's the danger of religion, it allows people to do that.*

Ironically, blood spilled throughout the history of violence against one another is never silent. The cries of blood and soul reach heaven, crying out to every succeeding generation to heed its voice and reconcile its suffering. Interesting, this vibrational sound of blood and soul is as old as time itself. There are two accounts of this phenomena recorded in the Bible:

> *Adam made love to his wife Eve, and she became pregnant and gave birth to Cain. She said, 'With the help of the Lord I have brought forth a man.' Later she gave birth to his brother Abel. Now Abel kept flocks, and Cain worked the soil. In the course of time Cain brought some of the fruits of the soil as an offering to the Lord. And*

James A. Houck, Jr., Ph.D.

Abel also brought an offering—fat portions from some of the firstborn of his flock. The Lord looked with favor on Abel and his offering, but on Cain and his offering he did not look with favor. So Cain was very angry, and his face was downcast. Then the Lord said to Cain, 'Why are you angry? Why is your face downcast? If you do what is right, will you not be accepted? But if you do not do what is right, sin is crouching at your door; it desires to have you, but you must rule over it.' Now Cain said to his brother Abel, 'Let's go out to the field.' While they were in the field, Cain attacked his brother Abel and killed him. Then the Lord said to Cain, 'Where is your brother Abel?' 'I don't know,' he replied. 'Am I my brother's keeper?' The Lord said, 'What have you done? Listen! Your brother's blood cries out to me from the ground. Now you are under a curse and driven from the land, which opened its mouth to receive your brother's blood from your hand.' Genesis 4:1-12

Elsewhere it is recorded:

When the Lamb opened the fifth seal, I saw under the altar the souls of those who had been slain because of the word of God and the testimony they had maintained. They called out in a loud voice, 'How long, Sovereign Lord, holy and true, until you judge the inhabitants of the earth and avenge our blood?' Then each of them was given a white robe, and they were told to wait a little longer, until the full number of their fellow servants, their brothers and sisters, were killed just as they had been. Revelation 6:9-11

Regardless of the geography, lands that have witnessed humanity's atrocities against one another have not only absorbed numerous blood-soaked traumas, but also the energy from such traumas have stained the souls of victims and perpetrators who have been unable to free themselves. In fact, few people realize that these souls are being continuously held in the *tar pits of traumatic energy* though ancestral stories, annual remembrances and celebrations that emotionally, psychologically and spiritually re-wound the souls of generation after generation. Today, as lovers of history, many people are caught up in the stories of how people died tragically at the hands of others. In fact, some of these stories often become sensationalized plots for movies and other forms of entertainment. Yet despite this awareness of humanity's stories, many people are often ill-equipped to offer any kind of solace for these souls (let alone their own) impacted by the energetic cycle of intergenerational trauma. The reason for this is because these stories are always told from a place of woundedness, and hardly ever from a place of healing.

As I sat there with my Native American Indian teacher in silence, looking at my bloody finger, my face became flushed with energy. His ancient words of *ancestors, blood* and *soul* sank deeper and deeper into the core of my own soul and made my heart beat louder. Suddenly, the Lakota phrase *Mitakuye Oyasin* (we are all related) awakened in me a sense that all life is intimately connected, cutting across all time and space. I became aware of the interconnectedness of all things on the level of the soul that exceeds a simple linear dimension of past, present and future. For me, this interconnectedness is more like a burst of light extending out into multi-dimensional and multi-generational soul relationships. In that moment, I no longer saw people as being divided by generation, race, gender, nationality, religion, language and culture; I saw all people as beautiful souls in physical bodies. In fact, within a split of a split of a second, the created elements (e.g., vegetation, animals, minerals, water, fire, earth, stars, the universe, etc.) formed an interconnected kaleidoscope in my mind. The reality of this interconnected and interdependent relationship that was once incomprehensible to me, now resonated a wave of clarity that also called me to listen carefully to the collective cries of the soul like I had never listened before.

Many theologians, scholars and scientists down through the centuries have struggled to espouse the most accurate definition of what the soul is, let alone, what is our relationship to ourselves? Therefore, without trying to muddy the scholastic waters, my definition of the soul is that *purest essence of ourselves that exceeds all physical, emotional and psychological limitations. Strip everything else away in our lives and it is our soul that is a divine mirror of the Soul of the Universe.* I believe the Judeo-Christian Creation story affirms this reflection:

> *This is the account of the heavens and the earth when they were created, when the Lord God made the earth and the heavens. Now no shrub had yet appeared on the earth and no plant had yet sprung up, for the Lord God had not sent rain on the earth and there was no one to work the ground, but streams came up from the earth and watered the whole surface of the ground. Then the Lord God formed a mam from the dust of the ground and breathed into his nostrils the breath of life, and the man became a living soul.*
>
> Genesis 2:4-7

The soul is not just something we have as a result of being created, but instead, the soul is who we *authentically* are. We are not merely bodies that have souls; we are divine souls who have bodies. In a sense, our mind and body provide form (e.g., *breath, matter and movement*) to our soul which is formless (Rael, 2015). Interestingly, as a reminder of this truth, Judeo-Christian Scripture notes the times when God (who is formless) dwelled in earthly form structures, e.g., the Tabernacle (Exodus 40:34) and the Temple (2 Chronicles 5:13-14). Furthermore, Christians also understand that the greatest example of God dwelling in form comes from the Gospel of John 1:14, *The Word became flesh and made his dwelling among us. We have seen his glory, the glory of the one and only Son, who came from the Father, full of grace and truth.* Even the Apostle Paul echoes this incarnational sentiment as he writes… *in Christ, all the fullness of God dwells in bodily form* (Colossians 2:9). Furthermore, as we read these scriptural passages carefully, we come to understand that Christ has given us examples through service, love, forgiveness, mercy, etc., how to live as soul in our everyday lives. Yet, we may still believe there is nothing more to us than our mind and body. After all, our physical nature strongly contends for our attention all the time in terms of hunger, thirst, fatigue, pain, sickness, procreation, etc. Ironically, we may often misunderstand an all-important lesson as we try to drown out the soul's cry for that divine connection, by focusing instead on what our egos are projecting in any given moment.

Nonetheless, it is the cry of the soul in each of us to fully realize that we are primarily souls, and we long to have that connection and reconnection with God. Regardless whether or not we have suffered trauma, paying attention to ourselves as soul, and listening to our inner cry, moves us out of the illusion that a mind/body consciousness rules. Important as they are, the mind and body are merely vehicles, if you were, to realize higher consciousness of soul. When we listen attentively to our soul's cry, we become aware that everything we truly desire can never be reached by the mind and body, because these are driven by ego, selfishness, fear, pain, pleasure, etc. This is not to say that the mind and body is all evil and the soul is all good. This kind of duality was what drove people in medieval times to punish themselves with physical wounds, believing that they could suppress the ego and physical desires, in order to become more righteous and holy in the eyes of others and God. Again, this is to misunderstand who we are as soul. We can never attain higher levels of God-consciousness through the mind and body because these forms are limited.

Indeed, one day our hearts will stop beating and our brain waves will cease, and the form will decay. The physical, emotional, and the psychological aspects of ourselves are earthbound and therefore, restricted in this sense. Once these physical cessations occur, we as soul are released to go back to God, the Creator and Sustainer of Life. However, for some souls this is not the case, at least not immediately. For example, there are unresolved tragedies and trauma that keep the formless soul trapped or bound here on earth. Since the body brings form to the formless soul, how might this explain unresolved traumas one has experienced in his or her earthly lifetime? Similarly, the study of *epigenetics*, which focuses on the bio-chemical changes that occur in our genetic codes as a result of traumatic experiences, is it possible that unresolved trauma also places a veneer of energetic suffering and anguish (e.g., *agony, shame, victimization, guilt, apathy, grief, powerlessness, revenge, darkness, fear, desire, anger, resentment, rage, bitterness, etc.*) so intense that it hinders the soul from moving beyond the place where the traumatic event occurred? I believed so, and thus, my journey began.

Listening to the Voices of Our Ancestors

One of my favorite places in South Dakota for spiritual renewal is *Mato Paha*, Bear Butte. In fact, I feel such a strong connection there that my Lakota friends call me, *Mato*. From the moment I first set foot on the mountain, I knew there was, and is, an element of great spiritual energy that touched me as a soul. I was on my second vision quest at the time, when I heard the words in my soul, *I live on!* Stunned, I did not know where these words came from, but they resounded repeatedly, *I live on…I live on…I live on!* As I continued to climb the mountain, the voice became stronger and stronger within me. Perhaps I was becoming sensitive to the voice of the mountain, i.e., from Native American Indian people and their ancestors who climbed this mountain for generations and generations. Perhaps it was the voice of my own soul. Nonetheless, it was a call to begin paying attention to the voice of my ancestors.

Bear Butte

Prayers Ties on Bear Butte

James A. Houck, Jr., Ph.D.

Since that time on Bear Butte, I have become more attuned to the rhythm of Creation; being attentive towards its annual cycles and resonating beat, if you will, that governs all life. This rhythm of life begins with our very first sound of our mother's heart beat inside the womb. We are comforted by this continuous *whoosh, whoosh, whoosh* reverberation that soaks into every fiber of our being. Daily, we are nurtured by the womb's warmth and nourishment, until the day we are born, when we are then thrust into all kinds of unfamiliar sounds, sights, and the pace of everyday life. Although we grow accustom to these new experiences, *circadian rhythms* are there to remind us of our connection to Life. For example, on a yearly cycle, there is an energetic rhythm that occurs with the change of seasons, from Spring to Summer to Autumn to Winter. Often, we recognize these changes in the rising and falling of temperatures, the migration of birds, the hibernation of bears, etc. Monthly, women experience the energetic rhythm of menstruation that assures the continuation of the human race. Daily, there are also energetic rhythms in the rising and setting of the Sun and Moon, high and low tides, even our sleeping and eating patterns are governed by energetic, rhythmic cycles. Ironically, there is even an energetic rhythm to our souls. The soul has a language that is spoken, urging us to discover our true selves. It is a language that reminds us that we are eternal souls, housed in a body (1 Corinthians 3:16-17). In fact, with every funeral and memorial service we attend, we are reminded that the only thing that lives on after our death is the soul. Everything physical about us either goes back into the ground or is surrendered to the flames. Only the soul continues beyond this world into the heavenly realms of the universe which far exceed our present comprehension. Many of our ancestors and relations knew this truth and lived their lives accordingly, but sadly many of them did not.

Each year as I visited Bear Butte, the call to listen to my soul was becoming more and more intense. Not only was I being called to listen in a unique way, but also called to help others discover their true selves. For example, I have counseled people in different pastoral and professional venues who want to heal from the family patterns of psychological brokenness, emotional pain, suffering and grief. They struggle with finding their own voice that empowers them to redefine who they are, despite their emotional, physical and spiritual wounds. For many, this struggle involves overcoming intergenerational wounds of family patterns of emotional sabotage, abuse, neglect, drug and alcohol dependence, chaos, anxiety, depression, co-dependency, suicide, stigma, violence, diseases, trauma; not to mention guilt, shame, feelings of inferiority, forgiveness and finding peace.

Ironically, the more I worked with wounded people helping them find the voice of their soul, the more I was discovering that the cry of the soul is not limited by time or space. In fact, recognizing this truth was part of my own soul's cry that had been with me from an early age. My first encounter with the supernatural came when I was around 10 years old. I was born and raised in the church and knew all about God, Jesus, the Holy Spirit, angels, etc. Yet little did I realize at the time the depth of the soul's cry to connect with God. For example, during one rainy Winter night I laid in my bed and listened to rain rhythmically drum against the window, lulling me to sleep. Suddenly I heard a strong, *tap, tap, tap* on the window. I rubbed my eyes awake and peered out the glass to see what was going on. There were no trees close by or birds awake at that hour, so I shrugged it off and went back to bed. Within minutes I heard again, *tap, tap, tap!* This time it was a little bit louder and more directed. Again, I shot up out of bed and looked to see if there was someone outside my window. Nothing. I stood there for a while and listened carefully as the rain continued to cascade down the glass, occasionally being illuminated by a flash of lightening. Finally, I went back to bed, determined to go to sleep quickly. No sooner had I pulled the covers over me and shut my eyes then there was that sound, *TAP, TAP, TAP!* This time very loud and more deliberate. I kicked off my covers and went to the living room where my parents were watching the news. *It sounds like somebody is outside tapping on my window! They keep going, 'tap, tap,*

tap!' Immediately my mother shrieked, *He's alive! Chet is still alive! He is hurt and sending out an S.O.S!*

My mother came from a large family; 12 brothers and sisters. She was the second oldest out of 12 and Chet was a year older than her. Chet loved to fly his Cessna plane whenever he had the chance. When we visited him in Massachusetts, he would take our family flying on Saturday mornings. Weeks before the *window tapping,* my uncle Chet had a very emotionally stressful day. Most people when they need to unwind after a stressful day would grab their keys and go for a drive. Instead, my uncle Chet went flying. He must have had engine trouble because according to the police reports, his Cessna crashed in a secluded area of dense forest. Search parties turned up nothing everyday they went out. What made matters worse was that everyday there were significant snow accumulations that often forced searches to be called off. For days and weeks there was no sign, no word, and hope was rapidly fading. My mother told me in a letter she received, that my grandmother's prayers to God were very simple during this time: She wanted her son to be found before she died. Weeks later her prayers were answered. The authorities found my uncle Chet's plane covered in snow and tree limbs. His body was recovered about a hundred yards from the plane where he died from exposure. Indeed, he was calling out for help, perhaps having only the strength to tap. In hindsight, a person could say that there were many rational explanations as to why the events occurred the way they did. In fact, one could certainly question why I heard his tapping instead of his wife or mother? Why not his son or daughter? Nonetheless, I know as a boy I still had plenty of questions. Today, I like to think that what I heard was an awakening to begin the healing process in the family.

Death has always been an interesting topic to discuss. No other subject, except for say, politics and religion, pushes so many of our physical, emotional and spiritual buttons. Whereas some people are fascinated by the topic of death, others avoid the mere mention of it, as if talking about death would *jinx* their life. Still, what I have discovered in counseling others is that the majority of people avoid death because they cannot bear the thought of being separated from loved-ones and friends. In other words, the gripping fear around death, loss and grief, can be an unrelenting vice that squeezes out life similar to Mauriac's *Vipers'* (2017). For as much as we are gripped by the fear of death, there is something even stronger, namely, the sound of our soul's cry to be connected and reconnected with God.

As a young boy, I believe God put this prayer in my heart to hear the cries of others. Whenever I would be in a crowd or part of a chaotic, cheering noise, the voices would blend together and sound like one collective painful cry. I thought I was going crazy, but soon discovered that I was not listening with my ears, but with my soul. Eventually, this cacophony soon became the foundation from which I would pray for others. Interestingly, down through the centuries, cultures and societies have also heard the voices of millions and millions of souls that not only cry from the depths of their trauma, but also cry out for justice, healing, redemption and peace.

CHAPTER TWO

It Takes a Village to Hide, Help and Heal Abuses

On a crisp sunny November morning, my Native American Indian friends and I drove from Philadelphia to the former site of the Carlisle Indian Industrial Boarding School. They were in town for a fundraiser and wanted to see this school, since their only knowledge of this place was from stories they had been told or read. Native American Indian Boarding Schools have always been a sensitive subject with my friends, as they recall the horrific stories told to them by tribal grandmothers and grandfathers when they were younger. Several of these experiences have plagued their ancestors with physical, psychological and spiritual scars that are a constant reminder of how the United States views their so-called *savage and uncivilized race.* Ironically, history's patterns of prejudice, cruelty, and mistreatment is not exclusive to Native American Indians, but also extends to any gender, race, class, ethnicity, nationality, etc., in which a society and its systems (governmental, educational, religious, science, etc.) categorized as unworthy, untouchable or unlovable. Today, many people look to place specific blame for such brutality, and yet, who is at fault? Who do you prosecute for such crimes against humanity? Can individuals be singled out, or does blame belong to communities in general? Just as the ancient African proverb states that it *takes a village to raise a child,* so too does it take a village to perpetuate physical, emotional and spiritual atrocities, no one acts alone. Surprisingly, Adolf Hitler acknowledged this phenomenon early in his life:

> *Even in those days, I saw that there was a two-fold method by which alone it would be possible to bring*

about an amelioration of these conditions. The method is: first, to create better fundamental conditions of social development by establishing a profound feeling of social responsibilities among the public; second, to combine this feeling for social responsibilities with a ruthless determination to prune away all excrescences which are incapable of being improved.　　　　Hess, 2015

Yet, as more and more of these historical atrocities emerge from those whose cries reach our own souls, villages may want to hide their heads in the sand and pretend not to see, hear, and speak no evil. However, the time has come that we can no longer pretend that we are not part of systems that produces and perpetuates the mistreatment of others.

Standing in the middle of the Carlisle Boarding School gravesite, we were struck by the diversity of the Native American Indian children we identified by their white gravestones. Among the children buried there were Cherokee, Lakota, Sioux, Inuit, Apache, Pueblo, Seminole, and many other tribal nations. About a third of grave stones were marked *Unknown*, representing unidentified children. As we blessed each grave with tobacco and sage offerings, we honored all who were buried there, by not referring to them as children, but instead, referring to them as grandmothers and grandfathers; ancestors. In this one prayer, we basically unraveled Captain Richard Pratt's (2004) philosophy of *killing the Indian to save the man.* Pratt's philosophy fueled a nation's behavior of assimilating Indians into European ways by forced relocating children, stripping them of their names, traditional clothes, hair, language, religion, and other native customs. Thousands of children were portrayed as having been assimilated into American culture in the historical picture sitting on the grass in front of Pratt's home and headquarters. As we stood on that grassy lawn, my friends were deeply moved as they proudly proclaimed through their tears that *Pratt had failed because we (Indians) are still here.* Yes, truth never stays buried because humanity cannot, has not, and will never be able to annihilate who people truly are, eternal souls.

Unknown Child's Grave
Carlisle Indian School

Carlisle Indian School Gravesite

Graves may acknowledge the lives once existed in a certain place and time, but the soul is not bound by time, space and dimension.

James A. Houck, Jr., Ph.D.

Graves may hold the remains of physical bodies that have been mutilated, charred, violated and hidden, but graves, marked or otherwise, have never been able to hold the soul. We live on. Therefore, when we look at our blood, we acknowledge those who have come before us and those who come after us. The evidence of our connectedness is in the soul and blood that holds the truth of not only what we *collectively* have been through, but also who we *collectively* are. I strongly believe that humanity is at a stage in its cycle that is being called to awaken to this truth and reconnect with God on a higher conscious level of soul.

The Carlisle Indian Boarding School

Established in 1879, the Carlisle Indian Boarding Industrial School, located in eastern United States was the first of its kind located outside the reservations. The School was modeled after the Hampton Institute for African Americans, which educated and trained African Americans to assimilate into society. Under the leadership of Captain Richard H. Pratt (1892), and backed by the U.S. government and religious organizations, the Carlisle School was held up as a model for all other schools that sought to assimilate Native American Indian children into productive Euro-Americans. Many people of that time-period believed that these boarding schools were also the most effective way to stave off a dying breed, as well as integrate the Native American Indian into a thriving Euro-American culture. Lakota Chiefs such as *Blue Horse, American Horse* and *Red Shirt* were among the first Native American Indians to send their children to the Carlisle School. These leaders were convinced that by learning the English language, customs and skills, was the only real future their children had in terms of survival (Rinaldi, 1999). Still, others like Lakota Chief *Red Cloud* and Sicangu Chief *Spotted Tail* mistrusted the white way of educating of Native American Indian children and were urged by Captain Pratt to comply with this new system. In a letter to Spotted Tail, Captain Pratt writes:

> *Spotted Tail, you are a remarkable man...you are such an able man that you are the principal chief of these thousands of your people. But Spotted Tail, you cannot read or write. You claim that the government has tricked your people and placed the lines of your reservation a long way inside of where it was agreed that they should be. You signed that paper, knowing only what the interpreter told you it said. If anything happened when the paper was being made up that changed its order, if you had been educated and could read and write, you could have known about it and refused to put your name on it. Do you intend to let your children remain in the same condition of ignorance in which you have lived, which will compel them always to meet the whiter man at a great disadvantage through an interpreter, as you have to do? As your friend, Spotted Tail, I urge you to send your children with me to this Carlisle School and I will do everything I can to advance them in intelligence and industry in order that they may come back and help you.*
>
> Pratt, (2004). *Battlefield and Classroom: Four Decades with the American Indian*

What astonishes me about this letter is not the persuasiveness of Pratt's words to Spotted Tail, but rather the insulting undertone of his letter implying that *if you (Spotted Tail) had been educated and could read and write, you could have known about it and refused to put your name on it.* Furthermore, in his haste to provide the United States with a prototypical school for others to follow suit, Pratt also galvanized a condescending perspective that would carry on for centuries. In other words, his arrogance disregarded the whole Native American Indian world view of his day, namely

- Strong connection to Creator and all created beings
- To stay connected to Creator in a relationship is to stay connected to and living according to nature's cycles and learn from animals how they raise their young, hunting, survival, etc.
- Honoring traditions of ancestors
- Ancestors are always part of the native way of life and perspective.
- Relationships are based on honor, respect and love.
- Family and ancestors are valued;
- Children are considered *wakan injan*, i.e., sacred, pure and holy.
- A continuation of the culture. (Deloria, 2003)

Everything and everyone is woven together into an all-encompassing world view. You cannot separate one thread from the woven fabric without unraveling the whole blanket (Ibid, 2003). In his letter, Pratt suggested that Spotted Tail learn the *white ways*, so he would not be taken advantage of, instead of dealing honestly with him. Why would Spotted Tail, or any Native American Indian, need to guard against being lied to unless, Pratt and others know how people will deceive the Native American Indian? Furthermore, it also implies that the burden of survival is placed on Spotted Tail, instead of Pratt reaching out in humility to understand native culture. From today's perspective, not much has changed since 1879, and then some. Just look at the protest against building the Dakota Access Pipeline (DAPL) in 2016. On February 22, 2017, Native American Indians and other environmental activists were forcibly removed and/or arrested, from their protest camps. Nonetheless, there are still people today who think they know what is best for Native American Indians who do not live on the reservations. What often makes matters worse is that the same type of people *represent* Indians in government, but never stop to listen with humility to the real needs of people. Today's egocentric approach simply continues what Pratt and others began.

Although admission to the Carlisle School was voluntary at first, it then became increasingly coercive. Native American Indian children were often taken away from their families by force. Anything less than a total assimilation of the Native America Indian into the Euro-American culture was not tolerated as set forth by Captain Pratt (1892). His philosophy of *kill the Indian, save the man* further pushed his egocentrism as this world view echoed throughout other residential schools in the United States and Canada:

> 'A great general has said that the only good Indian is a dead one,' Pratt said. 'In a sense, I agree with the sentiment, but only in this: That in all Indians there is a race that should be dead. Kill the Indian in him, and save the man.'
> (Official Report of the Nineteenth Annual Conference of Charities and Correction, 1892).

Native children were made to endure forced relocation to the Boarding School. In addition to being cut off from families thousands of miles away, their Indian names, rich with tribal significance, were changed to Christian names. Their long hair, also a part of tribal significance, was cut short, and all Native American clothing and accessories (beads, feathers, moccasins, etc.) were destroyed. The children were forced to read, write and speak English. For those children who attempted to speak their own language or follow their religion, they were punished with mouthfuls of soap. Living arrangements were also deplorable in that the children were forced into overcrowded rooms, and they had to endure exhausting lengthy work hours. Physical, sexual, emotional, and spiritual abuses occurred frequently at the hands of the educational and religious staff (Grisham, 2012). Because of harsh conditions with little to no medical care, many children ran away. Other children died from exposure to tuberculosis or small pox. Some children simply could not survive the pain of separation from their families, their health impaired by the school's strict routine:

> It is hard to imagine dying of homesickness. Yet it was a very serious problem for Indian students. 'Homesickness with them became a disease', wrote an official at Hampton Institute. 'Boys and girls actually suffered in the flesh as well as the spirit; could not eat, would not sleep, and so prepared the way for serious trouble. When people do not take care of their bodies, it becomes easier for them to become sick.' The profound sadness caused by homesickness weakened the students and made them susceptible to deadly diseases such as tuberculosis and influenza. These contagious diseases easily spread because of unsanitary conditions at the boarding schools. It was not unusual for dozens of students to sleep in one big room lined with rows of beds or for two children to sleep together in a single bed. This enabled germs to spread easily from child to child.   Cooper, (1999)

By the 1880s, there were 60 Indian Boarding schools throughout the United States. By 1900, thousands of Native Americans were living at 150 boarding schools around the United States. To the north, there were approximately 69 Residential Schools throughout Canada; and 80 Residential Schools by 1931 (CBC News, 2008). Ironically, the last federally-run residential school, Gordon Indian Residential School in Saskatchewan, closed in 1996.

Governments and religious orders such as Catholic, Anglican, Methodists, etc., were often seen as extensions of one another as, more often than not, extreme and cruel measures were taken by these systems to separate native children from their families, and to separate Native American Indians from their soul. Yet, as more and more lawsuits are coming out against the once government/religious established boarding schools, adult survivors are exposing the harsh treatment they received. Through their heartbreak and tears, many share how they were often physically beaten, whipped, burned, thrown down stairs, molested, exploited and raped by officials. In fact, adult survivors of childhood boarding schools also suffered emotional, psychological and spiritual abuse as many believed that they had been abandoned by God, because God's representatives were hurting them (Woodard, 2011).

The Mohawk Institute: Brantford, ON, Canada

Similar to the Carlisle Boarding School, the Mohawk Institute (established in 1829) in Brantford, Ontario was viewed as its model for other Canadian residential schools to follow. After previous and unsuccessful attempts to assimilate aboriginal children, the Mohawk Institute, led by John Brant, combined teaching trade skills with classroom academics and religion. Students were taught carpentry, weaving, tailoring and spinning to name a few (Miller, 1996).

Yet also like the Carlisle Boarding School, despite the attractiveness of equipping native children to become productive members of Canadian societies, there was more than meets the eye when it came to living at the Mohawk Institute, and industrial schools in general. Commonly referred to as the Mush Hole (because of the *not fit for pig consumption* mush children ate regularly), living conditions were deplorable as aboriginal children were exposed to harsh treatments. Russ Moses attended the Mohawk Institute from 1942-1947 writes:

> *Our formal education was sadly neglected; when a child is tired, hungry, lice infested and treated as a sub-human, how in heaven's name do you expect to make a decent citizen out of him or her, when the formal school*

curriculum is the most disregarded aspect of his whole background? I speak of lice, this was an accepted part of "being Indian" at the Mohawk – heads were shaved in late spring. We had no tooth brushes, no under-wear was issued in the summer, no socks in the summer. Our clothing was a disgrace to his country. Our so called "Sunday clothes" were cut down First World War army uniforms. Cold showers were provided summer and winter in which we were herded en masse by some of the bigger boys and if you did not keep under the shower you would be struck by a brass studded belt...

Mohawk Institute, Brantford, ON

By 1907: Dr. Peter Bryce, Medical Inspector for the Department of Indian Affairs, toured the residential schools of western Canada and British Columbia and wrote a scathing report on the *criminal* health conditions there. Bryce reports that native children are being deliberately infected with diseases like tuberculosis, and are left to die untreated, as a regular practice. He cites an average death rate of 40% in the residential schools. Despite the sub-par health conditions in the residential schools, there was also an underlying philosophy that promoted a more aggressive euthanasia of savage communities

(Rheault, 2011). By 1830, Canadian Indians were seen as a drain on the economy by the Crown of England, so it was believed that these people had to become productive through the means of evangelization, education and agriculture. The residential schools were the perfect tools for assimilating this race. Schools seemed harmless enough, but there is a huge difference between the schools and the educational systems they represented. For example, Miller, (1996) notes that educational systems in general were driven by three goals or learning outcomes:

- Explain to the individual members of a society who they are, who their people are, and how to relate to other people and the physical world around them.
- Train youth in the skills they need to be successful and productive members of their societies, and ultimately to the government.
- Instruct students to become properly socialized members who will share in collective values, provide for its needs, and defend its existence.

Despite its simplicity, it does not take a genius I.Q. to recognize the opportunity governments and religious orders possess to manipulate truth in order to exploit a people and push their own agenda. Furthermore, it also stands to reason that governments or religious orders can make education into anything they want it to be by distortions of truth or flat out brainwashing. For example, if you viewed Native American Indians as uncivilized savages, then you can design education to teach them accordingly. If you teach Indians who attended Boarding Schools that their religion, language, etc. is inferior to the white society, eventually what will students come to believe? If they are taught that they are incapable of making logical decisions for themselves, how long does it take to turn a group of people into dependents? Has much changed since then? How many of us in history classes were taught the perspective of Native American

Indians other than how colonization benefitted white Anglo Saxon people? This kind of coercive education, undergirded by physical, emotional, sexual and spiritual abuses, makes for a very powerful means to control the hearts and minds of any generation.

Generations and generations after the Carlisle Boarding School closed its doors in 1918, Native Americans are still here; still enduring the memories of the endless suffering of their people. Over 10,000 Native American children from 140 tribes attended the Carlisle Boarding School, but according to Hunt (2012) only 158 students graduated. Which leaves the question...*where are the others*? Mass graves of native and non-native people are being uncovered throughout the world. Generations and generations from other indigenous schools are coming forward with eye witness stories of abuse and deaths that have scarred both their memories and bodies. Government and ecclesiastical bodies scramble to offer apologies and comprise truth and reconciliation commissions to ease their consciences. However, apologies are not enough? Not when corrupt systems, illegal practices and entitlements are still evident today.

The ancient African proverb states that *it takes a village to raise a child.* In other words, the survival of any people extends beyond the immediate family. Regardless of nationality, creed and race, we are more connected to one another than what we realize. However, just as it takes many to contribute to the development of a generation of children, history now shows us that it also takes a village to hide scandals, abuses and atrocities. No one person or entity acts alone. No secret remains hidden, and truth never stays buried. Yes, dead men (and women and children) do tell tales of how they died. Some died of natural causes. Some died at the hands of others, and some people were not even considered worthy to be buried respectively. But for all these atrocities and more, it is time for us to begin telling the stories of how they lived. It is time for us to see them for who they are; souls. Souls that live on after their hearts have stopped beating and their brain waves ceased. Souls that surround us like a cloud of witnesses or communion of saints. Our ancestors are speaking to us constantly through the blood that runs through our veins. Yet, how do we reconcile these events with what we do today? This is the real effort behind healing intergenerational trauma.

Quite often, Native American Indians are forced to carry their scars on the inside, which are not so easily visible except for the explicit *Rez* behaviors of alcoholism, homelessness, drug use, crime and suicide. Yet if we look closely below the surface of these behaviors, we discover emotional and spiritual symptoms of boarding school trauma: hopelessness, depression, anxiety, mistrust, nightmares, sadness, hypervigilance, etc. Ironically, these symptoms are also appearing in native youth who are one, two, three, even four generations removed from such boarding experiences. This phenomenon, of course, leads to grapple with these questions:

- How is it possible that children, grandchildren and great-grandchildren are experiencing the same emotional, psychological and spiritual symptoms as their ancestors who experienced boarding-school related rape, murder, starvation, molestation, etc.?
- Are these children and grandchildren simply over-identifying with the stories communicated by their ancestors?
- Are traumatic experiences locked somewhere in the DNA of survivors, only to be passed down later?
- Are traumatic symptoms modeled from one generation to other?

How Did We Get Here? The Doctrine of Discovery

The emphasis of the *Doctrine of Discovery* (see Appendix A) was due to its dependence on the collaboration of the Church and State that cemented the fate of indigenous people. Popes gave their blessing and anointed these rulers and representatives as sanctified conquerors to confiscate, and control other lands of anything they discovered not already claimed by Christian rulers. In other word, the Catholic Church treated indigenous peoples as if they were animals; they had no (European) title to the land on which they lived. For example, 40 years before Columbus *sailed the ocean blue*, Pope Nicholas V issued to King Alfonso V of Portugal the bull Romanus Pontifex, *The Doctrine of Discovery*. This *Doctrine* specifically sanctioned war on all non-Christian people, and gave explorers such as Columbus, Cortez, Pizarro, Cook, Hudson and the rest, both legal and moral license to do whatever they wanted to the people and lands they encountered. These explorers not only carried the papal authority to conquer, colonize, and exploit all non-Christian lands, but also to capture, vanquish, and subdue the Saracens (Muslims), pagans, and other enemies of Christ, and take all their possessions and property (Davenport, 1917). This papal bull was often viewed as an extension of the socio-political-theological stance of the *Crusades*, medieval centuries of military campaigns designed to expand the territory of Christendom across Europe, Africa and the Middle East. Although these crusades stretched from the 11th to the 15th centuries, they had no shortage of crusader volunteers who were absolved from their sins, all the while, killing in the name of God those who did not follow Christianity (Ibid, 1917).

By the time Columbus sailed in 1492, he was authorized to take possession of any lands he discovered that were not under the dominion of any Christian rulers (Thacher, 1903). Furthermore, in 1493, Pope Alexander issued the *Inter Cetera* (see Appendix B), which granted Spain's Catholic King and Queen Ferdinand and Isabella, the right to conquer the lands which Columbus had already found, as well as any lands which Spain might discover in the future, including any people discovered in such land *to be subjugated and brought to the faith itself* (Davenport, 1917). This act ensured the Christian empire would continue to expand through brutal acts of genocide committed by Columbus and his men against the indigenous people of the Caribbean. Furthermore, these papal documents were frequently used by European conquerors in the Americas to justify an incredibly brutal system of colonization, *which dehumanized the indigenous people by regarding their territories as being inhabited only by brute animals.* (Story, 1833). In 1992 the Indigenous Law Institute spearheaded a movement to revoke *Inter Cetera*. Over 60 indigenous delegates drafted a *Declaration of Vision* at the Parliament of World Religions in 1994:

> *We call upon the people of conscience in the Roman Catholic hierarchy to persuade Pope John II to formally revoke the Inter Cetera Bull of May 4, 1493, which will restore our fundamental human rights. That Papal document called for our Nations and Peoples to be subjugated so the Christian Empire and its doctrines would be propagated. The U.S. Supreme Court ruling Johnson v. McIntosh 8 Wheat 543 (in 1823) adopted the same principle of subjugation expressed in the Inter Cetera Bull. This Papal Bull has been, and continues to be, devastating to our religions, our cultures, and the survival of our populations.*

Australia's Myall Creek Massacre:

In 1838, with a sense of entitlement to the resources of the land, British settlers were taking more and more of the Aboriginal lands of colonial Australia. Because these settlers feared being outnumbered by Aboriginal tribes, it was common practice to dispose of Aboriginal people as they saw fit. Gangs of stockmen, namely the *Big Bushwhack*, were known for specifically hunting Aboriginal families and raping Aboriginal women (Tedeschi, 2014). At one such place called the *Myall Creek Station*, stockmen herded defenseless Aboriginal people from their huts, hands tied together, 800 meters toward the top of a hill. Once they reached the top, Aboriginal people were hacked to death, beheaded and the bodies were left to rot. Two young girls were spared only so they would be raped later. Afterwards, it was told that the stockmen spent the night drinking and bragging about their killings (Ryan, 2008). After the *Myall Creek Massacre*, attacks on Aboriginal people increased, but became more discreet, as the British continued to poison food and bury the corpses of the Aborigines. In her work, *Massacres to Mining: The Colonization of Aboriginal Australia*, Roberts (2008) describes a little girl's account of the violence toward Aboriginal people:

> *My mother would sit and cry and tell me this; they buried our babies in the ground with only their heads above the ground. All in a row they were. Then they had tests to see who could kick the babies' head off the furthest. One man clubbed a baby's head off from horseback. They then spent the rest of the day raping the women, most of whom were then tortured to death by sticking sharp things like spears up their vaginas till they died. They tied the men's hands behind their backs, then cut off their penis and testicles and watched them run around screaming until they died. They killed in other bad ways too.*

To add further insult to injury, the Aboriginal Protection Act of 1886, empowered several Australian state-run institutions (e.g., Aboriginal Protection Board with the help of local law enforcement, British educational and religious systems) to force Aboriginal people of mixed descent, known as half-castes, to assimilate into British society. To achieve this assimilation, the Board did not implement a system to punish British whites for any future crimes against Aboriginal people, but instead, the state-run institutions took even more control away from Aboriginal people, namely their identity, family life and culture (Roberts, 2008). This new policy specifically targeted the removal of half-caste (one white and one Aboriginal parent) children from their mothers, placing them in a state/religious boarding school. It was assumed by the Board, that because of the increase of white settlers in the country, and the increase of half-caste children, the full-blood tribal Aboriginal population would be unable to sustain itself. A.O. Neville (1947), Chief Protector of Aborigines in Western Australia for 25 years, defends his attitudes and decisions toward the Aborigines in his work, *Australia's Coloured Minority: Its Place in the Community*:

> *I make no apologies for writing the book, because there are things which need to be said. So few of our own people as a whole are aware of the position [of Aboriginal]. Yet we have had the coloured man amongst us for a hundred years or more. He has died in his hundreds, nay thousands, in pain, misery and squalor, and through avoidable ill-health. Innumerable little children have perished through neglect and ignorance. The position, in some vital respects, is not much better today than it was fifty years ago. Man is entitled to a measure of happiness in his life. Yet most of these people have never known real happiness. Some are never likely to know it. The causes of their condition are many. Mainly it is not their fault, it is ours, just as it lies with us to put the matter right.*

The movie, *Rabbit Proof Fence* (Miramax, 2002) also tells a true story concerning three half-caste Aboriginal girls (14-year-old Molly, her 8-year-old sister Daisy, and their 10-year-old cousin Gracie), who were forcibly taken from their mothers in Jigalong by a local constable, and placed in the *Moore River Native Settlement*, located in northern Perth, Western Australia. However, only two of the three girls escape, walking 1,500 miles along a *rabbit-proof* fence to get back home. The movie underscores the traumatic physical, psychological and spiritual effects the Aboriginal Protection Act had on Aboriginal families at that time. The underlying theme of A.O. Neville as Chief Protector is evident throughout the movie, that the half-caste state of children must be bred out of them because Aboriginal peoples of Australia are a danger to themselves. Thus, by placing them in boarding-school like camps with other half-caste girls, they will eventually grow up to be laborers and servants to white families in society. If they should marry, it would be to only white men, and thereby the Aboriginal bloodline would diminish within a generation or two (McGregor, 1997). Aboriginal children were still being forcibly removed from their families throughout Australia until 1970. Pilkington (2013) refers to these children as the stolen generation.

Today we might be tempted to dismiss such treatment of indigenous people as an unfortunate time in United States, Canadian and Australian history. However, sadly the Doctrine of Discovery became the backbone of a way of life to this day. In particular, the Doctrine of Discovery further influenced the United States as seen in the 1823 Supreme Court case of *Johnson vs. McIntosh*, was a series of land disputes involving Illinois and Piankeshaw Indians. Previously, the land that is now the State of Illinois, was sold by the Illinois and Piankeshaw Indians to Thomas Jefferson, following the American Revolution. As a result, the land then became the property of the United States government, which was then sold to William McIntosh. The Supreme Court's decision held that Native American Indian tribes did not own absolute title to their lands, but instead held a *right of occupancy*. The tribal right to sell their land to non-Indians was restricted, with any transfer of land being illegal unless approved by the federal government (Law Libraries, 2016). Chief Justice John Marshall explained the Supreme Court's decision:

> *Christian European nations had assumed "ultimate dominion" over the lands of America during the Age of Discovery, and that – upon "discovery" - the Indians had lost "their rights to complete sovereignty, as independent nations," and only retained a right of "occupancy" in their lands. In other words, Indians nations were subject to the*

*ultimate authority of the first nation of Christendom to
claim possession of a given region of Indian lands.*
(Johnson: 574; Wheaton: 270-1)

Other historical examples of the Doctrine of Discovery include:

- Chief Justice Marshall legitimized the Doctrine of Discovery by citing the example of the English charter issued to the explorer John Cabot, as in order to document England's "complete recognition" of the Doctrine of Discovery (Johnson:576). Cabot was authorized to take possession of lands and disregard the Native American Indians who were there. Since the United States claimed independence from England in 1776, they were the successor nation who had a legitimate right to the land and basically ignoring the rights of native Americans and to claim that the "unoccupied lands", (i.e., land unoccupied by Christians) of America rightfully belonged to discovering Christian European nations. In this way, the United States government established its sovereign authority over Native American Indians by its own authority to have complete control in all matters.

- Cherokee Nation vs. Georgia of 1831: The United States government did not recognize any Native American Indian nation as free, and were viewed as *domestic dependent nations,* subject to the federal government's absolute legislative authority over the people and their lands (Berry, 2001).

- General Allotment Act of 1887: Since the United States ignore the terms of solemn treaties that they entered into with Native American Indians, 90 million acres of land were taken away from Native American Indians... *peacefully.*

- Indian Removal Act of 1835: Removed Native American Indians from their southern homelands east of the Mississippi River. More popularly known as the Trail of Tears (Perdue, 2003).

- <u>Violation of the 1868 Treaty of Ft. Laramie</u>: The United States government confiscated sacred land known as the Black Hills from the Great Sioux Nation. Previous, the *Treaty* recognized the Sioux Nation's exclusive and absolute possession of their lands.
- <u>Violation of the 1863 Ruby Valley Treaty</u>. The United States government paid the Secretary of the Interior $26,000,000 for 24 million acres of Western Shoshone lands. According to the government, because the Western Shoshone people refused to sell the land, they forfeited their rights to the land, since the government paid itself on their behalf (Chen, 2007).

Contemporary Impact of the Doctrine of Discovery

The doctrine of discovery, a concept of public international law expounded by the United States Supreme Court in a series of decisions, originated from various church documents in Christian Europe in the mid-1400s to justify the pattern of domination and oppression by European monarchies as they invasively arrived in the Western hemisphere. It theologically asserted the right to claim the indigenous lands, territories, and resources on behalf of Christendom, and to subjugate native peoples around the world.

Today, as a concept of public international law, the *Doctrine of Discovery* continues to be a source of contention between indigenous peoples and governmental systems who attempt to understand the *Doctrine's* impact. For example, the United Nations Permanent Forum on Indigenous Issues (2012) states:

> *Indigenous and native peoples spoke out against continued use of the internationally recognized principle of "terra nullius" which describes land belonging to no one but that could, in some cases, be acquired through*

occupation — as well as anachronistic norms, like the Regalian Doctrine, under which private land title emanates from the Spanish crown. Such principles were based on racist, unscientific assumptions, many said, and could not be used by States to justify the "theft" of native lands, territories or natural resources.

Others argued that the Discovery Doctrine — and its contemporary effect — should be studied by the Permanent Forum, as should indigenous legal systems to understand how they regarded its application. The term "conquest" should not be used in a manner to suggest that conquest had occurred. Echoing the comments of many, Steven Newcomb of the North American Caucus said the original free and independent existence of indigenous peoples — and their relationship with their territories — predated domination by western Christendom. That free existence was the source of their birthright.

To date, the *Doctrine of Discovery* has yet to be rescinded by the Vatican, although many petitions and open letters have been written. For example:

Your Holiness, this position as expressed in the Papal Bull has led to several ills in this world, namely Slavery, Unjust Treatment, Poverty, Discrimination, Apartheid, Separate But Equal Laws, Jim Crow, Financial Ruin, Massacres and much more. To justify the cruelty of slavery and subjugation of Africans, the slaveholders, for one, claimed that Africans were not human and therefore could be used and abused in any way the slaveholders so desired. This cruelty was for, as you know, the financial gain of slaveholders at the expense of others and the slaveholders very own humanity.

> *Many of the slave-holders also claimed to be Christian and obviously chose to accept the ongoing concepts of major doctrines, such as the Papal Bull of 1493, as a rationale for their behavior. As mentioned, people of color throughout the world still suffer from these ills. Historically, and in the 20th and 21rst centuries alone, all of this has been importantly coupled with countless reactions to this oppression such as Sit-ins, Marches, Occupy Movements and many other collective actions in the United States and internationally. Yet, the oppression You have declared 2016 as a year of Jubilee. Luke 4:18-19 states, "The spirit of the Lord is upon me, because he has anointed me to preach the gospel to the poor; he hath sent me to heal the broken hearted to preach deliverance to the captive, and the recovery of sight to the blind, to set at liberty them that are bruised, to preach the acceptable year of the Lord." I cannot think of a better way to honor this declaration of 2016 as a year of Jubilee than by a Papal repudiation of the "Doctrine of Discovery."* Beasley, (2016)

People who are aware of their intergenerational trauma often struggle to not only fight against being defined by its characteristics, but also find their struggle is against educational, judicial, socio-economic, correctional and health care systems. Among indigenous people, excessive poverty, teenage suicides that exceed other ethnic peoples, extreme incidences of Type II diabetes, high unemployment rates, etc. These examples are but a few of the contemporary cultural, communal, and individual damages experienced by indigenous peoples in the U.S., due to the generational impact resulted from the legacy of the Doctrine of Discovery.

The Hiawatha Asylum for Insane Indians.

It has been well established that the percentage of insanity is greater among half-breeds than among full-blooded Indians. That is explained by the theory of crossbreeding, that has a tendency to weaken the race. For this reason, it is confidently expected by those who have made a study of these conditions, that the rate of insanity will greatly increase as our civilization grows.

Senator R. Pettigrew (1897)

In 1898 the United States government passed a bill that created the Hiawatha Asylum for Insane Indians. Located in Canton, South Dakota, the Asylum would be the only federal mental institution in the United States created solely for the purpose of housing and treating American Indians who were purportedly mentally ill (Dilenschneider, 2013). Largely hidden from American history, the Asylum began receiving patients in 1903, and thereafter, Native American from various Tribes all across the U.S. were sent to the asylum. Hopkins (2011) notes that conditions there were shocking:

- The facility operated without power or indoor plumbing.
- It was exceedingly understaffed.
- One or two attendants looked after an entire ward of patients.
- Staff lacked medical training, supervision, and were utterly ignorant of native languages and customs.
- Physical abuse as a means of controlling patients was tolerated.
- Until 1926, matrons who worked at the asylum were not professionally trained nurses.
- Patients were often shackled to beds, pipes, or radiators and were forced to lie in their own filth for extended periods.

- Forced sterilization on patients.
- Patients at the asylum were showcased for the amusement of paying tourists who were invited there from all over the country.

Following the *Meriam Report: The Problem of Indian Administration* (Miller, 1928), the Commissioner of Indian Affairs called Dr. Samuel Silk, from St. Elizabeth's Hospital in Washington D.C., to investigate the institution further. What Dr. Silk uncovered was alarming. To say that conditions at the Hiawatha Asylum were inhumane is an understatement. Patients lived in squalor and food was not fit for human consumption. The air inside the Asylum was noxious, because windows were sealed shut and the chamber pots were left full of human excrement. Silk also discovered a woman lying in mounds of her own maggot-infested feces. Other patients had been locked away in isolation for years at a time. Silk also found a young boy locked up in a straightjacket, barely clothed and alone. Because the Asylum admitted Native American Indian children, often without parental consent, babies were born there although most did not survive (Joinson, 2016).

Perhaps the most disturbing finding of that Silk's investigation was that the majority of Native American Indians admitted to the Asylum did not suffer from mental illness. Although the Commissioner of Indian Affairs authorized all admissions to the asylum, those admissions were based on referrals from Indian Agents who supervised reservations. Some patients suffered from alcoholism, but most patients were sent to the asylum because they were considered *problem Indians* who opposed government interests or refused to give up cultural beliefs and practices. Further investigations of the Hiawatha Asylum also made national news. In 1933, The New York Times ran a story entitled: *"Sane Indians Held in Dakota Asylum: Patients Kept Shackled."* With national attention now on the inhumane conditions of the Hiawatha Asylum, the Indian Affairs Commissioner finally closed the Asylum's doors in 1934. Hopkins (2011) notes that as it turned out, the Hiawatha Asylum was just another means of instilling fear in natives, who were threatened with the prospect of being shipped off if they refused to obey or assimilate. Records show that at least 350 patients were detained at the asylum. To this day, there is no record of why any of the Native American Indians were placed there, or their causes of death.

Junipero Serra and the California missions

By the mid-18th century, Spain sought to extend its claims in northwest California, as well as strengthening defenses against the English and Russian empires who were seeking their own claims. This perspective was again seen as a divine rite since in 1493 Pope Alexander VI issued a law granting Spain's dominion over all lands that Columbus had located. In 1769, Spain sent Franciscan Fr. Junipero Serra to not only spread the gospel by building a series of missions along the California coast, but also to make the native Indians productive, loyal members of the new colony. Although Fr. Serra is given credit for building nine missions before his death, a total of 21 missions were built and remain to this day. Prior to Pope Francis canonizing Fr. Serra, the Vatican held firm in its belief that Serra was *a man of his time.* In fact, Fr. Serra helped Spain colonize California by converting thousands and thousands of Native Americans to Catholicism. On the other hand, for many descendants of Native American Indians, Fr. Serra was the one responsible for destroying their ancestors' traditional way of life. For example, in exchange for their labor, Fr. Serra promised Native American Indians abundant food and gifts, but they were quickly enslaved in these missions where they lived, worked and worshiped under the authority of Spanish priests and soldiers. Their whole native way of life, i.e., language, culture and religion were now stripped from them, in exchange for adopting Spanish ways of life (Castillo, 2015):

James A. Houck, Jr., Ph.D.

The goal of Christianizing the Indians was a failure, due largely to the Franciscan belief that it was unnecessary to teach the Indians proper Spanish, or for the friars (with a few exceptions) to learn the natives' tongues so they could fully explain Christian doctrine to the neophytes. When, decades later in 1833, the Indians were freed, many of them manifested their resentment and anger toward the friars by immediately casting aside their Catholicism. Further, the Spanish government required the teaching of Christian doctrine only in Spanish, and not in any native language.

In an interview with Vincent Medina, assistant museum director at San Francisco's Mission Dolores, Meraji (2015) recorded that native *people were enslaved in the missions. They were whipped if they spoke their language. If they tried to escape, they were forcibly brought back, flogged and punished, and kept in stocks. People were getting diseases. They were horrible places to be.* Noll (1992) further notes that this treatment reflected an attitude, common at the time, that missionaries could and should, treat their wards like children, including the use of corporal punishment. In his own letters, Fr. Serra in 1780 writes:

That the spiritual fathers [friars] should punish their sons, the Indians, by blows appears to be as old as the conquest of these kingdoms, and so general, in fact, that the saints do not seem to be any exception to the rule. Undoubtedly, the first to evangelize these shores followed the practice, and they were surely saints. . .In the life of Saint Francis Solano, who has been solemnly canonized, we read that, while he had a special gift from God to soften the ferocity of the most barbarous by the sweetness of his mission in the province of Tucumán in Peru—so we are told in his biography—when they [the Indians]

*failed to carry out his orders, he gave direction for his
Indians to be whipped by his fiscales.*

Castillo (2015)

The theme of *how many villages within the Church and State does
it take to hide histories of abuse, neglect and genocide,* continues to this
day when Pope Francis visited the United States in 2015 and officially
made Fr. Junipero Serra a saint at a Mass celebrated at the National
Shrine of the Immaculate Conception in Washington, D.C. Ironically,
to canonize a saint who was considered instrumental in American
history, as well as marking this ceremony in the American capital,
was hailed by some as a great day in the Catholic Church. In fact,
Archbishop Jose Gomez of Los Angeles, called the canonization of
Fr. Serra the *most important dimension of the Pope's visit to the United
States.* Others viewed the event as another example of how the Church
and State works together to perpetuate centuries of socio-economic
prejudices, oppressive attitudes and contempt for the weak. Moreover,
years prior to the Pope's visit to the United States, Catholic advocates
for Native American Indians around the country were asking the
church to not only recognize this terrible history in the church's past,
as well as to understand the concern indigenous people have for the
canonizing of such a figure. In an open letter to Pope Francis dated
February 24, 2015, Valentin Lopez, Chairman of the Amah Mutsun
Tribal Band, stated his disapproval for the canonization of Junipero
Serra because *the missions were brutal on Native Americans.*

*The reality of the California Mission system has yet to
be accurately taught in California schools or recognized
by the Catholic Church. Elementary school children tour
mission grounds and are taught that native people were
'docile and child-like savage pagans, saved by the kind
and benevolent padres'. In reality, the human remains
of thousands of indigenous people are scattered beneath
the grounds of the Missions that were built by Indian*

> *slaves as garrisons for the church and Spanish crown.*
> *Indigenous people died of rape, beatings and diseases*
> *introduced by the Spanish conquistadors in California.*
> *Spanish Priests did little to recognize indigenous people*
> *as humans and did not come to their rescue when women*
> *were raped by soldiers and settlers. With an over 90%*
> *indigenous mortality rate, Serra hardly 'saved many*
> *souls'.* Carac (2016)

The Rise of Eugenics

By the 1800s, the invention of better microscopes allowed scientists to discover the basic facts of cell division and sexual reproduction. Research then shifted to genetic understanding what really happens in the transmission of hereditary traits from parents to children. Gregor Mendel (1822-1884), a European monk whose research with plants basically outlined the principles of heredity, which he later applied to animals and people. Studying the separation of inheritable traits (e.g., flower color) in pea plants, Mendel observed that the flowers of each pea plant were either purple or white. Through the selective technique of cross-breeding common pea plants over many generations, Mendel discovered that certain traits show up in offspring without any blending of parent characteristics. Mendel's conclusions paved the way for society to understand the nature of human genetic inheritances such as chromosomes, traits, and diseases.

One such individual who studied Mendel's work was Sir Francis Galton, cousin to Charles Darwin. During Galton's time in the mid-19th century, there were two dominant teachings about human beings: One, as heartier races evolved over time, they would perfect society into a *survival of the fittest.* Inferior races would progressively become more impoverish, less educated and eventually die off (Spencer, 1852, 1995). Needless to say, many viewed the mixing of races as diluting superior races. For example, Grant (1936) echoed this sentiment that

*The cross between a white man and an Indian is an
Indian; the cross between white man and a Negro is a
Negro; the cross between a white man and a Hindu is a
Hindu; and the cross between any of the three European
races and a Jew is a Jew.*

The other popular belief among the elite class of England was
that most of society's problems (poverty, crime, illiteracy, etc.) of
the Industrial Revolution stemmed from certain groups of people
passing on inferior genes and thus producing social misfits as it were,
namely the Scottish and Irish (Black, 2012). To test this theory,
Galton studied the characteristics of upper class people in England.
These people were well educated, possessed strong dispositions,
rich, well-spoken, etc., all the admirable traits needed for a society
to stand head and shoulders over other nations. In his book, *Inquiries
Into Human Faculty and Its Development,* Galton (1883) coined the
term *eugenics,* which explained his theory that there was much more
to heredity than merely transmitting physical traits (hair color, eye
color, long or short legs, etc.) but also included passing on mental
and emotional qualities as well. Galton also went so far as to say that
he could improve the quality of certain inferior human populations
by discouraging reproduction of persons having genetic defects or
inherited undesirable traits. In fact, Galton promoted the belief that
He believed that humanity could help direct its future by selectively
breeding individuals who have "desired" traits. As a result, science
became the means to promote class hatred and bigotry; a *eugenic
crusade* as it were (Black, 2012).

It did not take long for Galton's beliefs to catch on in America,
who struggled with its own socio-economic issues in the dawn of
its Industrial Revolution. A zoologist named Charles Davenport,
intrigued by Galton's work on heredity and genetics, saw ethnic
groups as biologically different...*especially in their character, nature
and quality* (1935). Like Galton, Davenport also became obsessed with
race mixing, and often criticized America for its melting pot mentality,

James A. Houck, Jr., Ph.D.

which he saw as a result of stubborn, isolated inbreeding. Funded by the Carnegie Institution, Davenport set out to study the science behind evolution and established a *Biological Experimental Station* at Cold Spring Harbor in New York. There, Davenport convinced many influential people in society of tackling a bigger problem, namely the negro race. In a letter dated May 3, 1903, Davenport updated the trustees of the Carnegie Institution regarding the progress of Cold Spring Harbor:

> We have in this country the grave problem of the Negro... A race whose mental development is on the average, far below the average of the Caucasian. Is there a prospect that we may through the education of the individual produce an improved race so that we may hope at last that the Negro mind shall be as teachable as elastic, as original, and as fruitful as the Caucasians? Or must future generations, indefinitely, start from the same low plane and yield the same meager results? We do not know; we have no data. Prevailing opinion says we must face the latter alternative if this were so it would be best to export the black race at once.

As a result of this letter, Davenport was able to convince the American government to eliminate the inadequate and unfit. Now the emphasis was to search throughout the nation to methodically identify exactly which races were qualified to continue, and which ones were not. It is worth noting, that at this point in American history, science became involved in documenting so-called human genetic defects in other races and ethnic groups, but not their achievements (Black, 2012).

To secure such evidence, Davenport sought eugenic records in 42 institutions for the feebleminded, 115 schools and homes for the deaf and blind, 350 hospitals for the insane, 1,200 refugee or refuge homes, 1,300 prisons, 1,500 hospitals and 2,500 arms houses. (*Report on Committee on Eugenics,* 1910). Within this Report, Davenport had all the necessary data at his fingertips to be able to justify his scientific theories on inferior races. Furthermore, Davenport's classification defined feebleminded nests linked with epilepsy, cases of severely retarded individuals who cannot care for themselves, shyness, stuttering, poor command of the English language, and even nonverbal regardless of their talent and intellect. Epilepsy seemed for persons with epilepsy, seemed to be targeted as a mental weakness as it was believed that epilepsy was in the genes, and therefore this mental weakness was passed on from generation to generation to generation. (*Growing up, I remember my mother telling me stories that when she was a little girl, how she would often be scolded by teachers and mistreated by friends for having epilepsy. On occasion, she would have a seizure in class which often then led to her being shunned by friends, ridiculed by neighbors, and causing her to carry a baggage of shame which was not hers to carry for many years*). Again, we see how the most vulnerable in society, that is, those who are weak vulnerable susceptible to diseases, illnesses were taken advantage of by those in power; those who defined illness and made the roles.

As a result of Davenport's work, once the people who were of lower genetic quality were found in places of institutions, houses of charity, and so forth were identified, it did not take long for those in charge of the medical community to insist on forced sterilization laws. These laws not only prevented the feebleminded from reproducing more of their kind, but also, spare society from bearing the burden of their behavior or cognitive limitations. This forced sterilization also extended to people who were being released from prison, in order that they would not be able to reproduce more of their kind. Nonetheless, state legislation began to enact their own forced sterilization laws on the feebleminded. In 1905 Pennsylvania's legislature passed the *Act for Prevention of Idiocy* which empowered surgeons to perform operations for the prevention of procreation. Other states such as Michigan, Indiana, Illinois, Oregon, Washington, California, Nevada, Iowa, New Jersey, and New York followed suit.

Virginia seem to be one place where forced sterilization really took its toll on the people following World War I (Black 2012). Virginia was considered the *collecting place* for people who were poor, uneducated, diagnosed with epilepsy, feeblemindedness, and others who were considered morally unfit by the state. In 1914, Albert Priddy submitted a report to the General Assembly entitled *Mental Defectives in Virginia*, proposing large scale sterilization in state institutions for people who fit the above criteria (Lombardo, 2010). This Report led to the passage of Virginia's *Eugenical Sterilization Act of 1924*, which immediately targeted feebleminded women of child-bearing age, from 12-45 years old.

Carrie Buck's Story

Carrie Buck was 17 years old when she became first person to be sterilized under the *Eugenical Sterilization Act*. Both Carrie and her mother, Emma Buck, had previously been committed to the *Virginia Colony for the Epileptic and Feebleminded* with the diagnoses of feeblemindedness. Carrie was sent to this asylum after she had given birth to an illegitimate child; the result of being raped by a relative to her foster parents. Officials at the Virginia Colony believed that Carrie and her mother shared the hereditary traits of feeblemindedness and sexual promiscuity, which were sure to be passed on to Carrie's daughter, Vivian.

The decision to sterilize Carrie was challenged in the lower courts, citing a violation of the Fourteenth Amendment to the U.S. Constitution:

> *No state shall make or enforce any law which shall abridge the privileges or immunities of citizens of the United States; nor shall any State deprive any person of life, liberty, or property, without due process of the law;*

*nor deny to any person within its jurisdiction the equal
protection of the laws.*

In the trial of *Buck verses Bell*, the United States Supreme Court
upheld Virginia's sterilization law by a vote of 8 to 1. The high court
ruled that the state's law allowing forced sterilization of *any patient
afflicted with hereditary forms of insanity, imbecility, etc... for the greater
welfare of society*, did not violate the Fourteenth Amendment's equal
protection under the law. Moreover, Chief Justice Oliver Wendell
Holmes, Jr. justified the Court's decision by citing *Jacobson v.
Massachusetts* (197 U.S. 11, 1904), which upheld a Massachusetts law
requiring school children to be vaccinated against smallpox. Chief
Justice Holmes also laid the groundwork to rationalize such future
sterilizations with his statement:

> *It is better for all the world, if instead of waiting to
> execute degenerate offspring for crime, or to let them
> starve for their imbecility, society can prevent those who
> are manifestly unfit from continuing their kind...three
> generations of imbeciles are enough.*

Virginia's Eugenical Sterilization Act of 1924 became the model
for the United States, as sterilization rates increased and the categories
of people that qualified for sterilization were gradually broadened
to include criminals, prostitutes, and the homeless (Moore, 2004).
It is estimated that between 7,200 and 8,300 people were sterilized
in Virginia from 1927-1979. Twenty-two percent of the individuals
sterilized were African Americans, and two-thirds were women.
Many of those sterilized were not even told they were being sterilized,
but instead given some other explanation for their operation. All in
all, the legitimizing sterilization for certain groups led to further
exploitation, as group divisions were made along race and class lines
(Wong, 2013). Still, forced sterilization continued to be funded by

the American government, and was quickly becoming part of the American landscape (Garcia, 2013):

- *First Bill Proposes Sterilization for "Undesirables" (1849)*: Gordon Lincecum, a famed Texas biologist and physician, proposes a bill mandating the eugenic sterilization of the mentally handicapped and others whose genes he deems "undesirable." The bill is never brought to a vote (Disability Rights, Texas, 2010).

- *Indian Health Services (1973-1976)*. A study by the *U.S. General Accounting Office* finds that 4 of the 12 Indian Health Service regions sterilized 3,406 American Indian women without their permission between 1973 and 1976. The GAO finds that 36 women under age 21 had been forcibly sterilized during this period despite a court-ordered moratorium on sterilizations of women younger than 21 (Lawrence, 2000). Indian Health Service had "singled out full-blooded Indian women for sterilization procedures." In total, it is estimated that as many as 25-50% of Native American women were sterilized.

- *Skinner vs. Oklahoma (1942)*: The *Skinner vs. Oklahoma* case made it illegal for some lower class felons to be targeted for sterilization. The Supreme Court stated that *strict scrutiny of the classification which a State makes in a sterilization law is essential, lest unwittingly, or otherwise, discriminations are made against groups or types of individuals in violation of the constitutional guaranty of just and equal laws* (Williamson, 316 U.S. 535).

- Sterilization of Puerto Rican Women Reaches 30% (1965): In a predominately Catholic society where birth control was illegal till 1930, sterilization practices left 30% of the women unable to have children by 1965. The earliest governor of Puerto Rico is cited as saying that there were too many unskilled laborers, and not enough jobs in the island. This long sterilization campaign resulted in this practice becoming the birth control of choice for Puerto Rican women (Garcia, 2013). Instead of providing Puerto Rican women with access to alternative forms of safe, legal and reversible contraception, U.S. policy promoted the use of permanent sterilization. Misinformation, for women in general, was a common tool; women are often told that their status, namely related to immigration, housing, government benefits, or parenting, will be negatively impacted if they do not consent to the procedure. Many women are told that the procedure is temporary or reversible.

- <u>Nixon Administration Funds Sterilizations (1970)</u>: Following the passage of the Family Planning Services and Population Research Act of 1970, the Nixon administration widely offers sterilization of low-income Americans, primarily women of color. Independent reports would later indicate that many of the doctors performing these procedures do not follow informed consent protocols, deeming the sterilizations *involuntary as a matter of practice* (Ibid., 2013).

- <u>20,000 Operations Performed in California (1909-1979)</u>: California played a central role in the sterilization programs in the United States. Stern (2005) notes that Mexican-Americans and African Americans were disproportionally represented in the percentages of sterilization, and that this was rationalized by concerns about bad parenting, population burdens and even as *a punishment for bearing illegitimate children or as extortion to ensure ongoing receipt of family assistance.*

Eugenics Worldwide Impact

As sterilization laws were changing the moral landscape of the United States, eugenics was gaining worldwide traction in Europe. In 1912, the first of several *International Congresses of Eugenics* were held discuss implementation of programs to improve heredity (Bruinis, 2006).

Yet still in its infancy stage of understanding eugenics, Germany followed the American model of biological criteria for sterilization candidates, incarceration for socially inadequate people, and on-going debates on euthanasia. Citing America as his legislative precedent, Germany's Adolf Hitler soon became a strong advocate for the use of force to sterilize and the eliminate so-called *inferior races*. America's model seemed to be the missing piece Hitler needed to complete his vision for a superior race (Hess, 2015). In fact, German scientists, including Josef Mengele, were sent to America to learn how perfect their sterilization knowledge and skills (Mengele did indeed perfect his sterilization skills as he was later found guilty of conducting inhumane medical experiments on concentration camp prisoners at Auschwitz). By 1934, Germany led the way in eugenics and forced sterilizations, exceeding 5,000 procedures per month (Black, 2012). Ironically, even though American newspapers and broadcasts reported these atrocities being committed against non-Anglo-Saxon, and other so-called inferior people, many denied knowledge about what Germany was doing after World War II had ended. Again, the amalgamation of religious prejudices, science and government became a very powerful *three-pronged attack* on the weak and vulnerable of society (Ibid, 2012).

During the *Nuremberg Trials* (1945-1949), many of those who committed such eugenic genocide during World War II were confused and outraged as crimes against humanity charges were brought against them. Interestingly, they argued that what began as an American acceptable medical practice (*since 1907 sterilization laws had been passed in 29 states of the United States*), was now being condemned in German scientists who were trained by the Americans. Furthermore, those on trial for their crimes even quoted the 1927 United States' Supreme Court's decision *Buck verses Bell* in which Supreme Court Justice Oliver Wendell Holmes, Jr. uttered his famous phrase, *three generations of imbeciles are enough*. Nonetheless, out of the 24 Nazi doctors, scientists and soldiers on trial, 12 were put to death, nine were imprisoned, and three were acquitted. To bring further closure to an ugly time in world history, as well as internationally vowing never to let something like the Nazi genocide to ever happen again, the United Nations approved *Resolution 96* (see Appendix C) which added the definition and practice of genocide into International Law in 1946. Article II of this document states:

> *Genocide means any of the following acts committed with intent to destroy, in whole or in part, a national, ethnical, racial or religious group, as such: (a) killing members of the group; (b) causing serious bodily or mental harm to members of the group; (c) deliberately inflicting on the group conditions of life calculated to bring about its physical destruction in whole or in part; (d) imposing measures intended to prevent births within the group; and (e) forcibly transferring children of the group to another group.*

In the above historical examples listed by Garcia (2013), it appears that, despite the acceptance of the United Nations *Resolution 96*, the United States and other nations continued to sterilize groups of people, especially women, perhaps believing that since it was science, it could be justified. Yet despite this international law, sterilization abuses continued as women in the United States, and beyond its borders, have historically been subjected to coordinated efforts to control their fertility without their consent. For example, (Krase, 2014) cites that Latina women in Puerto Rico, New York City, and California were specifically targeted by the government for sterilization throughout the 20th century. In addition, North Carolina performed 65 percent of sterilization procedures on black women, even though only 25 percent of the state's female population is black. Furthermore, Native American women were subjected to coercive population control practices through much of the 20th

James A. Houck, Jr., Ph.D.

century. The *Indian Health Service*, functioning under the control of the United States Public Health Service, began providing family planning services to Native American families in 1965. Instituting similar practices to those experienced in Puerto Rico, as many as 25% of Native American women between 15-44 years old were sterilized by the 1970s (Ibid., 2014).

CHAPTER THREE

When Trauma Crosses Generations

When you dismiss my story, you dismiss who I am;
you diminish me.

Robert I. Sutton

Log onto any news journal today and in no time, you can find multiple stories of physical, emotional, psychological and spiritual trauma that have been linked to tragic and catastrophic events. From trauma centers in hospitals to the mental health field that specializes in trauma recovery, trauma has become an all too familiar household name. In fact, nothing tests the faith, courage and resiliency of humanity like an unexpected, unprepared and unexplained event that can leave people physically broken, psychologically or emotionally overwhelmed, and spiritually wounded. Yet despite advances in public awareness and academic research, trauma is still a misunderstood soul-phenomenon; a term often bantered about without fully comprehending its effect on generations of individuals and societies.

The Limbic System: Thalamus, Amygdala, and Hippocampus

Before launching into further discussion on trauma, I believe it is always beneficial to first explore not only how we are hard-wired to perceive our experiences, but also how and why some experiences remain unprocessed and encapsulated in our mind and bodies. As a result, when our memories (real and/or imagined) of traumatic experiences remain blocked, our interpersonal and intrapersonal relationships are always negatively affected. The reason for this effect on our relationships is because we interpret how we view ourselves, others and the world, through a distorted lens of trauma.

In the mental health and pastoral professions people who experience something stressful or traumatic are always encouraged to talk about it. We often hear, *let it out* or *talk about it…you'll feel better,* as we try to make sense of what has happened to us. However, depending on the severity of the experience, we may have difficulty being able to put into words or actions what has happened to us. Granted, we may still be in shock over the traumatic experience, so talking about a situation may take some time. Nevertheless, there will come a time when our bewilderment lifts, but we still lack the words to make sense of our traumatic pain. Although our minds may be capable of replaying the experience over and over, it is through communicating what has happened to us through stories, symbols and song creates a healing context for all generations.

The benefit of communicating our traumatic experience is to cause a psychological shift to occur in the mid-brain between the Amygdala and the Hippocampus. For example, initially, all information comes into our brains from what we see, hear, smell, taste, touch and intuitively. The data then enters the Thalamus, which relays this information to the prefrontal cortex area of the brain. The only sensory information that is not relayed by the Thalamus, is information related to smell. Scent is regulated by the Hippocampus, which is the most powerful organ we have in retrieving memories. The Hippocampus is also responsible for creating new memories, especially autobiographical memories (Bremner, 2006). For example, just think of how many times our memories are triggered by the scent of a loved-one's perfume or cologne? Perhaps our fond memories of childhood are triggered when we smell fresh baked cookies, or other smells around certain holidays. Of course, scent can also trigger unpleasant memories too, such as the smell of a perpetrator's perfume or cologne. Perhaps not so fond memories of childhood are triggered when we smell burning flesh, or other smells around certain holidays. Nevertheless, if what we experience is new information, the Thalamus then determines if it is a threat to us, while the prefrontal cortex determines the best course of action. However, if the information is anything closely resembling a past trauma, the Thalamus is triggered to interpret the information as a traumatic event, through the lens of the past. Previous traumas may be anything related to a life-threatening experience, the untimely death of a loved-one, being bullied in school or at work, feeling shame/guilt for not living up to another's expectations, etc. If a memory of a past trauma is triggered by a certain smell or odor, then the Hippocampus relays all this information. Based on the Thalamus' and/or Hippocampus' interpretation, signals are sent to the Amygdala, which regulates our emotional response to any experience appropriately, such as feeling happy eating our favorite food, or becoming nauseated if we smell blood. If the information is viewed as a previous trauma, the Amygdala creates a disproportionate emotional response (e.g., anxiety, fear, numbing, dissociation, etc.).

During these split seconds of interpretation, signals are also being sent to the Brain Stem, which gets us ready for action through the release of cortisol and adrenaline. As a result, our pupils dilate, our heart-rate increases, and we perspire. On the other hand, the Amygdala wants to interpret everything from the template of past emotional and physiological interpretations. When we experience a traumatic event, the Hippocampus and Amygdala vie for the control over how we may or may not process a life-threatening experience. For example, we could be sitting in an office and hear screeching tires off in the distance. Immediately, this sound may trigger a memory from a time when we were in an accident. We might automatically assume that someone is terribly hurt, or feel like we are reliving our own accident, because this is what happened to us. Our muscles tense and our stomachs churn. We may even re-experience pain in the body where we once had a physical injury from an accident (Van der Kolk, 2015). In reality we are in an office, safe and sound, but our emotional and physiological reactions are telling something us different; we do not feel safe nor sound. This reaction, all the while we are in a safe environment, indicates that we have unprocessed trauma.

Chipping Away at Resiliency

Indeed, the history of humanity has often been riddled with traumatic experiences. Physical, emotional, psychological and spiritual injuries have been well documented throughout the ages. In earlier times, perceptions and behaviors perceived by society to be odd or eccentric, described as humanity's *madness*, may have actually been an inability to cope with prolonged physical, emotional or psychological illness and distress. For the most part, I believe people can handle their daily stressors, cope with anxiety, and manage situational depression in healthy ways. In fact, people are able to excel at these coping mechanisms, because they have built up an internal hardiness. Call it wisdom, faith, perseverance, etc., these traits not only enable people to learn from the majority of their negative experiences, but also, they have learned to thrive and go beyond or transcend their so-called physical, psychological, emotional and spiritual limitations. Moreover, having resiliency means much more than rising above *that which does not kill me*. In its original context, resiliency means the ability to return to an original state or form after being bent or compressed (Moore, 2014). For example, if something is stretched, we would say that its resiliency lies in its elasticity, i.e., by recovering its original shape…like a rubber band snapping back after it has been pulled. In mental health circles, we have many images of resiliency that distressed people often are encouraged to become like, e.g., a willow tree; something that can bend even in the strongest storms, but not break. Long before much scholarly research was done on resiliency, martial arts expert Bruce Lee (1975) encouraged people to be *like water*. He states that water is a substance that fits into any container yet has the power to maintain its property (H2O) even as a liquid, solid and gas. It is this fact that water is able to adapt to any situation without being destroyed, which makes it an excellent object lesson for resiliency.

Yet do these images of a rubber band and willow tree capture the very essence of resiliency when it comes to our physical, emotional, psychological and spiritual losses? Not quite. The rubber band and willow tree do possess a degree of elasticity, i.e., being able to stretch and bend when met with an external force. However, what is often overlooked is that we are forever shaped by our losses and traumatic experiences, and as a result, can never *go back to way things were*. We may be able to *bend* during an emotional storm, but we never retain our original shape. For example, Van de Kolk (2005) states that

> There is a mistaken notion that trauma is primarily about memory—the story of what has happened; and that is probably often true for the first few days after the traumatic event, but then a cascade of defenses precipitate a variety of reactions in mind and brain that are attempts to blunt the impact of the ongoing sense of threat, but which tend to set up their own plethora of problems. So, trying to find a chemical to abolish bad memories is an interesting academic enterprise, but it's unlikely to help many patients. It's a too-simplistic view in my opinion. Your whole mind, brain and sense of self is changed in response to trauma.

For every change people experience in their lives they also experience a sense of having lost someone or something they once had. This is the basic definition of bereavement. Most people I have counseled want to hit the rewind button and go back to the way things were before they experienced pain, loss, and even trauma. Although this is a reasonable request, going back to the way things used to be is not even possible, because our losses shatter our assumptions and perceptions about ourselves, others and the world we in which live. In other words, everything we have known up until that point now

James A. Houck, Jr., Ph.D.

has been altered. We simply cannot look at our world through the same lens. Instead, by broadening our understanding of resiliency, we recognize our potential to adapt, persevere and change *in* the present moment. We all have this ability. We become more aware of this capacity when our resiliency grows as a result of hindsight, which in turn, prepares us for other moments in which we must adapt and persevere. To illustrate this point, Wilma Mankiller, first female chief of the Cherokee Nation, once remarked, *cows run away from the storm while the buffalo charges toward it – and gets through it quicker. Whenever I'm confronted with a tough challenge, I do not prolong the torment, I become the buffalo.* All of us need to recognize that such strength lies within. Unfortunately, some people only define themselves by their negative experiences, misunderstanding the language of resiliency, and thereby perpetuate a defeatist attitude that dictates their outlook on life.

As stated before, I am a firm believer that humanity possesses incredible resiliency. In fact, at times we have to be reminded of our inner strength and perseverance. Given enough time, support and encouragement, we can handle most anything that comes our way. We might even surprise ourselves, and others, just how resourceful we are. Nevertheless, even though we have our shining moments when we can rise to the occasion, we also have our breaking points when we can no longer keep ourselves together due to the inability to the withstand the relentless assault on our inner resources. Still, physical, emotional and psychological pain can be excruciating at times, but when we embrace our true selves as soul, we find the strength to rise above the pain. This is because pain and suffering are associated with the mind and body, and therefore, limited. Perhaps we all know of people who suffer tremendously with physical pain and ailments. Their bodies are racked with agony on a daily basis. Yet, within them there is a sweet disposition; a healthier outlook and a beautiful soul that can never silenced by the physical and emotional.

*Therefore, we do not lose heart. Though outwardly we
are wasting away, yet inwardly we are being renewed day
by day. For our light and momentary troubles are
achieving for us an eternal glory that far outweighs them
all. So we fix our eyes not on what is seen, but on what
is unseen, since what is seen is temporary, but what is
unseen is eternal.*   2 Corinthians 4:16-18

General Adaptation Syndrome

Hans Selye (d.1982) was an endocrinologist who first coined the term *stress*, as *the non-specific response of the body to any demand for change* (1974). His theory focused on the physiological or biological changes that are produced when a person responds to his/her environment. In other words, stress is our body's way of responding to a threat or challenge. For example, when confronted with a challenge, our sympathetic nervous system activates our survival *fight-or-flight* response. Once the threat or challenge has passed, the parasympathetic nervous system eventually returns our physiological reaction to a normal state of homeostasis. Initially, Selye conducted his experiments on laboratory animals to determine how they would react to acute physical and emotional negative stimuli (e.g., blaring light, deafening noise, extreme temperatures of heat or cold, starvation, perpetual confusion or frustration, etc.). As a result, all of the animals exhibited similar physical changes such as stomach ulcerations, shrinkage of lymphoid tissue, enlargement of the adrenals, heart attacks, strokes, etc. Inevitably, Selye became convinced that similar prolonged stimuli had the potential to cause the same diseases in humans. Call it stress, compassion fatigue, burnout, etc., our reaction to any stress-filled event leads us toward a three-stage bodily response and has the potential to overwhelm our well-being. Selye coined this model the *General Adaptation Syndrome,*

James A. Houck, Jr., Ph.D.

which contains three distinct phases that describes our physiological response to stress:

- *Alarm Stage*: As we perceive a stressor, our body reacts with a *fight-or-flight* response and our sympathetic nervous system activates the body's resources in order to meet the threat or danger. When of mind identifies the stressor as a threat or danger to our well-being, it immediately activates its fight or flight response system, and releases stress hormones such as adrenaline, noradrenaline and cortisol.
- *Resistance Stage*: As our bodies attempt to return physiological functions to normal levels, we remain on alert against the stressor. In fact, when a stressor persists, our body's defenses become weaker. More and more of our energy needs to be allocated in order to the repair damaged muscle tissues and lower the production of the stress hormones. Although the body has shifted to this second phase of stress response, it is not as strong as it was during the initial response.
- *Exhaustion Stage*: If the stressor continues beyond our capacity, the body's resources become exhausted, and this is when we become susceptible to illness, disease and even death. In other words, the body begins to lose its ability to combat the stressors and reduce their harmful impact, because the adaptive energy has all been drained. This stage eventually leads to people experiencing emotional burnout, or compassion fatigue in their everyday work.

Today, research on the physiological factors associated with stress have evolved beyond the Seyle's *fight or flight* phenomena. For example, Bracha (2004) expanded Seyle's understanding to include the stages of *freeze, fight, flight and faint*: For example,

- <u>Freeze</u>: When you are walking along a trail and you hear *rattling* noise. You look down but may not see a snake hiding in the grass. Your first response is to freeze because the amygdala detects an attack and signals the brainstem to inhibit movement. This reaction happens in a flash, automatically and beyond conscious control. We shift into a state of vigilance against any attacks and/or look for a means of escape. At this stage, the body is primed for fight or flight, although this may not be the next course of action.

- Flight: We see the snake slithering toward us and we quickly look for ways to remove ourselves from this threat, e.g., we back away or run away.

- Fight: If we have no means of escape from the snake, we will perhaps pick up a stick and fight, e.g., pushing the snake away to avoid becoming bitten, thus staying alive.

- Faint: If both flight and fight are futile, we may be gripped with terror to the point of shutting down and dropping to the floor. Opossums actually do this quite well. In a sense, the body goes into survival mode, decreasing heart rate and slowing growth. There is physical paralysis, and if things get worse, we may faints in hopes that our simulated death will prevent our actual death. (Narvaez, 2014)

Trauma: Transient Reaction or Intrusive, Persistent Re-Living?

Today, although stress has become a familiar word, its effects have influenced people on a physical, emotional, psychological and even spiritual level. Add to your stress an experience that is sudden that overwhelms our sense of well-being, and that is the making of a traumatic experience. These experiences can be life-threatening, real or imagined, and can knock the wind right out of us, physically, emotionally and spiritually speaking. The length of time it takes for us to get back on our feet, replenish our resiliency and rebuild our faith and philosophical beliefs that have been shattered by the crisis/trauma, speaks to the intensity of the traumatic experience. For example, *Acute Stress Reaction* (ASR) is a transient response to overwhelming physical and emotional stress that typically diminishes within a few hours or days (Friedman, 2015). We may have experienced ASR when we need to complete a task before a deadline, such as filing taxes, homework assignments, cramming for exams, or completing job-related projects. Other examples may include being in a minor car accident, interpersonal difficulties at work, or students having academic problems in school. During these times, and depending on our level of resiliency, we may experience rising heart rates, sweating, feeling dazed, shallow breathing, difficulty concentrating, etc. However, once the situation has been resolved, and perhaps through the additional help of our family or community support, our symptoms of ASR typically diminish.

Nonetheless, there are times when despite our ability to cope, exposure to real or perceived life-threatening events, overwhelm us for longer periods. Initially, *Acute Stress Disorder* (ASD) develops typically within one month of exposure to a traumatic event. Such events include, war, rape, sexual violence, molestation, sexual abuse, physical harm such as an attack, kidnapping, being taken hostage, terrorist attacks, torture, bombings, natural disasters and life-threatening accidents. Furthermore, first-responders also experience ASD when they are dispatched first to a scene of an accident or to collect human remains (Bryant, 2016). For the most part, a person with Acute Stress Disorder will experience symptoms (flashbacks, nightmares, emotional distress, impairment, altered sense of reality, hyperarousal, etc.) as soon as 3 days following a traumatic experience.

Post-Traumatic Stress Disorder

Initially, *Shell Shock* and *Combat Fatigue* were diagnosed exclusively in large numbers of American combat veterans who were seeking treatment for the lingering effects of exposure to war (Johnson,

1999, Linden, 2017). Yet, over time the definition and symptoms of Post-Traumatic Stress Disorder (PTSD) expanded to demonstrate the complexity of traumatic symptoms. This development allowed for specific ways of treating people who survived extremely painful experiences such as torture, rape, genocide, bombings, earthquakes, hurricanes, volcano eruptions, work-related machinery explosions, airplane and automobile accidents, *verses* people who experienced normal, but sometimes unexpected transitions of life, namely divorce, failure, marriage, rejection, serious illness, significant changes in finances, etc. All in all, the key to understanding what makes PTSD so unique to treat is that, although most people have the ability to deal with ordinary stress, sometimes their coping abilities are overwhelmed when experiencing a real or perceived life-threatening situation.

In 2013, the American Psychiatric Association revised the PTSD diagnostic criteria in the fifth edition of its *Diagnostic and Statistical Manual of Mental Disorders* (DSM-5). For the first time, the *DSM-5* now included a preschool subtype of symptoms for children ages four through six years old. This subtype is important to note because although PTSD has been widely reported in children and adolescents, younger children are often exposed to many types of traumatic experiences, such as physical, emotional, and/or sexual abuse, accidents, surviving a natural disaster, being bitten by animals and/or an invasive medical procedure (Philo, 2015). As a result, children will often reenact traumatic experiences through aggressive play with their toys or friends because this behavior provides them a sense of emotional relief, as well as the fact that their coping and cognitive skills are still developing (Cohen et al, 2017). For adult survivors of traumatic events, avoiding thinking and/or talking about such topics is common because of feeling overwhelmed. For example, some people may resort to ingesting alcohol or other substances as a way to numb their feelings/thoughts related to the trauma. Others may resort to forms of self-harm, e.g., burning, cutting, etc., that releases endorphins to either numb their feelings of trauma or creates a sense of feeling alive (Ferentz, 2014).

Complex PTSD

Over time, the recent descriptions of PTSD failed to capture some of the more emerging human experiences, there was a need to widen the net even further to include personal captivity, psychological fragmentation, the loss of a sense of safety, trust, and self-worth, as well as the tendency of people to be *re-victimized*. All in all, a distinct *complexity* was emerging in the field of trauma studies which included a person's loss of a clear sense of self. This unique type of loss as a result of a traumatic event goes much deeper than simply how we and/or others view ourselves. It also includes how a traumatic loss contributes to a sense of feeling disconnected from all relationships resulting in a loss of our core beliefs about who we are? Furthermore, when we lose our sense of who we are, we are perhaps more willing to seek out a sense of self- worth from others, thus allowing them to define us according to their definitions and expectations (Alger, 2014).

By expanding this definition of PTSD, today's health care, mental health and pastoral professionals are now able to better understand how a prolonged exposure to trauma, affects the psychological well-being of people in their everyday lives. I also assert that much of the intergenerational trauma can often be traced back to prolonged exposure to traumatic events, especially with the emphasis on the loss of a sense of self so prominent in surviving generations. Herman (2015) proposes Complex PTSD is a more complete diagnosis in order to not only describe the symptoms of long-term trauma, but also to provide specific mental health treatment options. For example, during prolonged traumatic experiences, people are typically held in a state of captivity, physically, emotionally or both. In these situations, people feel under the control of the offender and believe that they will never be able to escape from danger. Such examples of such complex traumatic situations include, being held captive in a concentration or prisoner of war camps, prostitution or child exploitation rings, prolonged domestic violence and/or prolonged physical, emotional, sexual abuse in children.

Residential School Syndrome

To the above examples of Complex-PTSD, I would also include exposure to residential boarding school living conditions that is defined as *Residential School Syndrome* (Robertson, 2006; Schaverien, 2015). Residential School Syndrome characterizes thousands of indigenous adult victims and survivors who attended government established and religious based residential schools as children. Although many survivors report symptoms that are similar to Complex-PTSD, e.g. depression, anxiety, addiction, suicidal inclinations, rage, and mental illnesses, the cause of their trauma is unique. For example, since the majority of native children were either forced to attend these schools by the government, or their parents were tricked into sending them with promises of improving their odds of survival, adult-children of residential schools often struggled with internalized feelings of abandonment, disenfranchised, oppression, shame and racism (Chrisjohn et al, 1994, Duffell et al, 2016).

The cause of such historical trauma that characterizes adult-children of the residential boarding school system is what Dr. Mary Ann Jacobs, Chair of American Indian Studies at the University of North Carolina at Pembroke, describes as being related to a genocide of a people. She notes that:

> *Where some major event is aimed at a particular group because of their status as an oppressed group. It could be a war; it could be cultural, such as when a people's language is banned and they are not allowed to speak*

*or print it. It could be the desecration of monuments,
such as graveyards and other sacred sites. Any of those
events that have to do with ignoring the humanity of a
group and having that part of social policy, be it formal
or informal, where it's not a crime to do that.*

(Coyle, 2014)

Lakota Indian Walter Littlemoon (2009) also shares his memories
of a childhood spent in a federally-imposed school system that did
everything else but educate, including stripping away of his sense of
self as a Native American Indian:

*The word 'education' is something that my mother had
agreed to, but that isn't what we got. It was almost like a
re-education camp where we were supposed to be turned
into something else that we weren't. So, we were always
called being uncivilized... or we were savages.*

Clymer, Indiana County, PA

Appalachia is a 205,000-square-mile territory of the United
States that follows the backbone of the Appalachian Mountains from
southern New York to northern Mississippi. It includes Virginia,
West Virginia, Georgia, Kentucky, Maryland, Mississippi, New York,
North Carolina, Ohio, Pennsylvania, South Carolina, Tennessee, and
parts of Alabama. Appalachia is made up of mostly rural communities
whose economies are primarily dependent on coal mining, forestry,
agriculture, chemical industries, and manufacturing. is a natural
resource that provides us with affordable energy. Visit any coal mining
town in Appalachia, and you hear the stories of personal struggle,
going to church, raising families, miner strikes, black-lung diseases,
heartbreak and tragic deaths. Such communities are all too identified

by their histories that have been etched out by the hard work of their backs, sweat of their brows and the tears of remembrance.

My father's side of the family raised their families in such a place in the western part of Pennsylvania. He was raised in a small coal mining town called Clymer, in Indiana County. Clymer appears to be like any other sleepy little coal mining town, but it did have its share of mining strikes and accidents as was typical with all kinds of mining activity in a town back in the day. What marks small town tragedy is something that was not just experienced on an individual level, but rather entire communities experienced trauma collectively:

> *At 1:00p.m. on August 26, 1926, a gas explosion was heard in the mine; 6 minutes later there was another explosion afterwards. By 2:00p.m. relatives and friends had gathered near the mouth of the mine causing heartrending scenes as the injured and the dead were being removed. Some looking for fathers, others their brothers and husbands, hoping against hope that each trip made out by the rescue crews would bring their loved ones back alive. Search rescue teams from all parts of Indiana and nearby counties appeared on the scene with their rescue apparatus taking turns descending into the mining clearing away the debris the bodies were hauled to the surface and electric cars and were wrapped in burlap before they were transferred to ambulances a long line of ambulances sent here from a dozen nearby towns… by the late afternoon rows of white shrouded figures lay in and provost morgue in a Clearfield Bituminous Coal Corporation machine shop. Most of the bodies were badly mutilated which made identification difficult.*
> The Indiana Gazette, Tuesday, October 5, 1926

My Grandmother never talked about that tragedy, apart from the news reports. She would have been a teenager at the time and may have been kept away from the site. Ironically, years later she married my Grandfather who worked in the same mine and was killed by a falling rock. My father was two years old at the time, and although he may have grown up without a father, he had plenty of collective trauma of the town to keep him company. Many people struggle to make sense out of tragedies, as a search for blame is their missing piece of an historical trauma's puzzle. Still, the horrific details of a natural disaster quickly call into question our assumptions regarding how fragile life is. I can only imagine the fear that my grandmother held in her heart each day when my grandfather crawled into that mine. I'm certain both of them knew the risks involved, but perhaps had no other means of *eking out* a living. Gas explosions causing cave-ins and other kinds of tragedies, are all too familiar scenarios for people living in coal mining towns.

A key aspect to understanding trauma is when a precipitating event overwhelms a person's well-being, e.g., a physical accident, near-death encounter, or even having to say goodbye to a loved-one's anticipated or unexpected death, the event is deeply etched in a person's psyche. However, since no two people experience events the same way, what could be described as a traumatic event by one person, could be described as a minor inconvenience to another. For example, suppose 100 people experienced a thirty-second earthquake. All 100 survivors would report something different based on their personal perspectives from their lived experiences. For some, this may have been their first experience of an earthquake, and they may not be sure if their reaction is appropriate: *What if there is another earthquake? Will I be ready? Will I be trapped? Will others be able to find me?* For others, this earthquake may have triggered memories of previous earthquakes, playing on their worst fears of experiencing pain, dismemberment, death, etc. Days, weeks, months or years later, people may feel as though they are still *physically* and *emotionally* trapped, although all signs of the earthquake have long passed. Still, these feelings are legitimate to the survivors for they people are, in a sense, trapped…*on the inside.* The energy of the trauma is being held somewhere in the mind and body, unable to be processed. Such people may feel overcome with feelings of suffocation, overcome with feelings of abandonment, overcome with feelings of being lost, even overcome with feelings of sorrow. Davis (2016) notes that as soon as a person judges or labels their inner pain as something bad or something they do not want or do not like, they are inadvertently and unwittingly holding onto their pain, thus preventing it from being processed in a healthy way.

For the most part, trauma is not a catastrophic event, but rather trauma is an *after-effect* of a perceived or real life-threatening situation(s) that measures our ability to survive, and thrive, in everyday life (Herman, 2015). To differentiate trauma, we might experience because of life threatening events verses trauma we might experience from significant life transitions, Van der Kolk (2005) categorizes trauma into the categories of *Big T* and *Little t* trauma. *Big T* trauma can be understood as experiences such as war, life threatening illnesses, violence, physical, sexual and/or emotional abuse, natural disasters, etc. With such experiences, there is an element of vulnerability to our personal safety and emotional well-being. *Little t* traumas fall into the context of everyday or transitional experiences, such as being promoted or fired at work, moving to another city, beginning or finishing school, changes in the family, getting married, etc. Although there is not an element of threat to our personal safety, *Little t* traumas have the potential to be just as overwhelming as *Big T* traumas, especially if unresolved traumatic life issues have been accumulating over time.

From a psycho-spiritual viewpoint, there is a huge difference between *Big T* trauma that results from natural disasters (e.g., fires, floods, earthquakes, etc.) verses experiences that have the potential to produce characteristics of both *Big T* and *Little t* trauma simultaneously. Such experiences would include direct physical, emotional and spiritual harm that is the result of the malicious intent of others. For example, within hate crimes and genocide, there are also components of justice and accountability. When people responsible for inflicting harm against others are not held accountable, or systems that continue to oppress people are not corrected, traumatized people are more likely to collapse from the additional layers of internalized humiliation, disgrace, shame, ridicule, etc. What makes matters worse is that these physical, emotional and spiritual wounds often remain *infected* when others are suffering similar pain and exploitation. In fact, when such atrocities, suffering, and oppression continue to be met with silent indifference or willful disregard, societies become numb to the fact that they encourage convenient justification of oppressive systems generation after generation after generation. In other words, when crimes against humanity are left unchecked, they not only serve to further cement trauma, but also send a dangerous message to other societies that such crimes can be committed in the future without consequence. Ironically, the potential is there in that crimes against humanity can produce a trauma which not only stains the soul, but also blindsides future generations with the emotional, psychological, physical and spiritual baggage of the past.

Yet what effect does trauma have on us as souls? Most of the time, we talk about the symptoms of grief and trauma in the language of the physical or emotional terms. Furthermore, if the spiritual component is explored in terms of *rebuilding faith and philosophical beliefs that are challenged by a loss* (Doka, 2002), the soul often gets lost in religious language. For example, on one hand, it is good to alleviate symptoms, as the majority of people I work with say how they just want to feel better, eat better, sleep better and be in healthier relationships. Yet on the other hand, what if we embrace true ourselves, as soul, and begin to transform the energy of our traumatic experiences through the voice of the soul? This is where things get a little interesting because in order to understand ourselves as soul, we must first suspend our logical, linear thinking. Ever since the Age of Enlightenment, we have been trained to verify experiences via our senses, e.g., *how much does it weigh, what does it look like, is it behavior predictable, can we place its role in our finite human understanding?* Yet, our souls simply do not play by those rules. It can never be grasped from a linear understanding of the mind; never has been and it will never be. Still, those who are looking for empirical evidence of the soul believe that unless the soul can be verified by this temporal template, the soul, then, does not exist. In fact, another important aspect when it comes to understanding trauma's effect on a soul, is that a person's soul is not mortal. The soul is the only thing that lives on after our hearts stop beating and our brain waves cease. The soul lives on eternally in other dimensions and timelessness in a *location* we are told is heaven, where the fullness of God exists in unfathomable glory, majesty and splendor.

Sustained History of Forced Migration of Children

Like intergenerational trauma, the effects of a historical trauma are far reaching. While certain historical trauma may be traced back to colonial times, it still can be felt today if the system has not been corrected. For over 400 years, the United Kingdom has used forced child migration as a key part of policy to take care of children whom they deemed as unwanted by society. From 1618-1970, over 130,000 children were removed (most without parental consent) from the United Kingdom to Canada, New Zealand, Zimbabwe and Australia (Child Migrants Trust, 2016). Again, it appears that although society was aware of this practice, it abdicated its responsibilities of child care to the government and religious institutions:

> It was a social policy which involved the transfer of abandoned youth from the orphanages, homes, workhouses and reformatories of the United Kingdom to overseas British colonies - later to the self-governing Dominions. Once overseas, the children were placed with colonial employers - usually in rural areas. Often the children were placed in local institutions for preparation and training prior to employment. The care and removal of the children was under-taken by religious

> *and philanthropic organisations...but with government*
> *approval and under the law as it then stood.*
>
> (Coldey, 1995)

However, it was not until perhaps the movie *Oranges and Sunshine* (2010), also published as *Empty Cradles* in 1994, that exposed the atrocities committed against these children, that societies started to pay attention to its role in the British government's scheme of forced child migration. *Oranges and Sunshine* focused on the years between World War II and 1967, when approximately 7,000 homeless children from England were shipped off to Australia and Canada. These children, who in the eyes of the government *were not going to be missed anyway*, were promised better lives in Australia; lives that would be characterized by oranges and sunshine. Now, many of these adults who spent their childhood in Australia, wanted to connect with their families. Their stories caught the attention of Margaret Humphries, a social worker from Nottingham, England. Initially, she began to hear stories about adults who were orphaned at a young age, raised in a religious boarding school atmosphere, and longed to reconnect with who they are through any surviving relative. Yet, as these stories unfolded, so too did the underlying issues of physical, emotional and spiritual trauma. The more Humphries investigated, the more she uncovered a tightly woven spider-web of government, education, and religious systems of boarding school experiences that traumatized so many of her clients. For example,

> *When _____ arrived, he was dispatched to a Church*
> *of England boarding school in _____. Other*
> *child migrants were less fortunate. Many ended up in the*
> *care of the notorious Christian Brothers where they were*
> *treated as slave labor and suffered horrific physical and*
> *sexual abuse. One victim told an official inquiry that his*
> *Christian Brother carers competed to become the first to*
> *rape him 100 times._____ escaped such trauma – he*

would be beaten with a strap if he did anything wrong. There's an emptiness in me. There always has been and I think the only thing that could fill it was her, my mother. Anyone would've thought there's a fella who's got everything, but it was like I had a block of ice inside me. I felt empty. I knew I was missing something. I couldn't work out what it was. And there was this feeling – I didn't know who I was. I didn't know where I'd come from. I didn't belong to anybody. I was in this void.

In an article entitled, *I can still hear the kids' screams,* Chenery (2011) interviewed a survivor, who was sent to Australia when he was a boy:

Life at Bindoon, run by the Catholic Church's Christian Brothers, was a catalogue of cruelty, where beatings and sexual assaults were daily events. Bindoon was nothing more than a pedophile ring. Most of the brothers were into raping and molesting little boys, sometimes sharing their favourites with each other. The boys were put to work building the series of grand buildings that Bindoon became. It was slave labour. Many of them are now deaf or partially deaf because they were constantly bashed around the head. He recalls children resorting to stealing food from the pigs they tended, because the pigs were better fed. Brother _____, the head of Bindoon, would eat bacon and eggs in front of boys who were fed porridge mixed with bran from the chicken feed. The boys would raid the bins for his scraps.

Furthermore, Chenery (2011) notes that children and adults who experienced a prolonged period (months to years) of chronic victimization and total control by others, may also experience the following difficulties:

- *Emotional Regulation*. May include persistent sadness, suicidal thoughts, explosive anger, or inhibited anger.
- *Consciousness*. Includes forgetting traumatic events, reliving traumatic events, or having episodes in which one feels detached from one's mental processes or body (dissociation).
- *Self-Perception*. May include helplessness, shame, guilt, stigma, and a sense of being completely different from other human beings.
- *Distorted Perceptions of the Perpetrator*. Examples include attributing total power to the perpetrator, becoming preoccupied with the relationship to the perpetrator, or preoccupied with revenge.
- *Relations with Others*. Examples include isolation, distrust, or a repeated search for a rescuer.
- *One's System of Meanings*. May include a loss of sustaining faith or a sense of hopelessness and despair.

Intergenerational Trauma's Impact

I prefer to define *Intergenerational Trauma* (IT) as *the increasing, and often relentless, psychological-physiological-spiritual re-wounding that, because of a traumatic experience, becomes unconsciously handed down to future generations through distorted perspectives, emotional illnesses, maladaptive behaviors and co-dependent relationships.* In fact, regardless of the historical context, what makes IT distinct from trauma in general is the fact that the psychological-physiological-spiritual re-wounding is the direct result of *premeditated acts of aggression, annihilation and/or negligence from a person (or persons) against another person (or persons)*. IT also includes direct and indirect human aggression against another, such as through oppressive political, social-economic, educational and religious systems. Furthermore, what often adds burning salt to these intergenerational wounds is the underlying theme of an omission of guilt by the offender(s). In other words, no system-changing olive branch has ever been extended to heal the wounds afflicted by those who stand guilty. However, when such attempts are made to acknowledge the past or offer forgiveness, its well-intended attempts to assuage the guilt from those associated with crimes or tragedies, is often seen as cold and offensive. This reaction should not come as a surprise because apologies often divert public attention away from understanding how contemporary policies continue to perpetuate and reinforce oppressive systems.

Buffalo Creek Disaster

In February 1972, the West Virginia Buffalo Creek Hollow recorded one of the deadliest floods in the United States. A *slurry dam*, owned by the Pittston Coal Company, located on the side of a mountain-top removal process, collapsed and sent 130 million gallons (equivalent to a 25-foot tidal wave) of watery sludge and other debris, crashing into the town below. Approximately 118 people were killed instantly, 1,000 people were injured, and over 4,000 people were suddenly homeless. This disaster was truly beyond comprehension, because unlike other coal-mining disasters that affected only the workers in the mines themselves, this time those affected and killed were families who were sleeping during the early morning hours.

A *slurry dam* has a distinct purpose in the process of strip-mining, or mountain-top removal: Before coal can be used for fuel, it must be washed to separate it from fragments of soil and rock. In a sense, the more impurities a company can remove from coal, the higher its market value. As a result, the *washing process* generates huge volumes of liquid waste, while the *mining process* generates millions of tons of solid waste. The cheapest way for coal companies to deal with these wastes is by constructing dams from the solid mining refuse to impound the liquid waste in the heads of valleys, close to their coal processing plants. These coal sludge impounding ponds have the capacity to store billions of gallons of liquid coal waste, *slurry*, containing water, rocks, mud, carcinogenic chemicals used to process coal, and toxic heavy metals that are present in coal, e.g., arsenic, mercury, chromium, cadmium, selenium, and others (SouthWings, 2016).

These chemicals have been known to leak from unlined slurry ponds into groundwater and nearby streams, thus contaminating water supplies to surrounding communities. Before any mountaintop removal operation begins, coal companies are required by law to disclose all environmental risks involved to the people in surrounding towns, such as uninhabitable landscapes, forests and wildlife habitats at the site of the mine, the loud sounds of the strip-mining machinery, hazardous living conditions, potential for water contamination, and *slurry* that prohibits anything from growing on the land (US Environmental Protection Agency, 2016). With all of these hazards, it is a wonder that anyone in nearby towns would approve of mountaintop removal productions. However, Stern (2008) notes when a community is continuously beat down by a system, they often feel like they have no voice and have no cause to complain.

In the days, weeks, months and years that followed the Buffalo Creek Disaster, survivors of this disaster often suffered severe mental anguish, as well as slow recovery from physical harm and financial loss. When the Pittson Company offered quick cash settlements to the victims, they were criticized for taking advantage of vulnerable people who may have still been dazed, no access to legal counsel, or fully knew the extent of their physical and/or emotional injuries. What added insult to the communities was that when the Pittson Company was sued, their main defense was that they could not be held accountable due to excessive rainfall that weakened the slurry dam, and therefore, they considered the disaster an *act of God* (Erikson, 1976).

When communities experience collective trauma, recovery and healing is often a very slow process. This due to the fact that because the emotional, mental, physical and spiritual wounds often evolve the means by which people not only identify themselves, but also can be used to exclude others who have not experienced the same trauma. In fact, there is often a shared traumatic psychological effect by a group of people and/or societies. However, for people who did not experience an event first hand, any psychological-physiological-spiritual effects are often passed on, thus experiencing symptoms of trauma, vicariously. For example, during World War II, the submarine *USS Puffer,* came under several hours of depth charge attack by a Japanese surface vessel, until the ship became convinced the submarine had somehow escaped. At a much later time, psychological studies were performed on the original crew. Results found that any new crewmen transferred to the *USS Puffer* were never accepted as part of the original team (Garrigues, 2013, Updegraff, Silvler and Holman, 2008). Later, US naval policy was changed so that after events of such psychological trauma, the crew would be dispersed to new assignments.

Traumatic events witnessed by an entire society can stir up collective sentiment, often resulting in a shift in that society's culture and mass actions. Well known collective traumas include, but are not limited to:

- Cathar Genocide
- Slavery of African Americans
- The Nazi Holocaust
- Dzungar Genocide
- Stalin's Great Purge
- The Armenian Genocide of 1915
- Selk'nam Genocide
- Massacre at Wounded Knee, South Dakota
- The Estonia Disaster in Sweden
- The Rwanda Genocide
- The My Lai Massacre
- Darfur Genocide
- The Belgium Congo
- The Nanking Massacre
- The assassination of world leaders

- Isaaq Genocide of 2014
- The shooting tragedy on Kent State University in 1970
- The India Partition of 1947 and the Kashmir Massacre
- Cambodian Genocide and the Khmer Rouge
- The September 11th attacks on the World Trade Center, the Pentagon and the crash of Flight 93.
- Etc.

At these sites, memorial placards and/or statues are often erected to constantly remind people of the community loss. Although well intended to *never forget,* these reminders make moving beyond the traumatic event almost impossible for some people, especially when annual observances often stir up feelings of pain, unresolved grief, and feelings of helplessness. Instead of empowering people to transcend this energy of emotional and psychological wounds, trauma is in avertedly passed on to succeeding generations. These generations may take on such trauma, vicariously, because of their indirect involvement through community associations, blood ties, and other affiliations such as integrated systems. For example, anthropologist Merida Blanco developed an unpublished intergenerational diagram that accounts for the effects of colonization violence on subsequent generations in South America. Levine & Kline (2006) note that Blanco's diagram can be traced directly to the history of Indigenous Australia:

- 1st Generation: Men who were killed, imprisoned, enslaved or in some way, were unable to provide for their families.
- 2nd Generation: The majority of men abused alcohol and/ or drugs to cope with their loss of identity and diminished sense of self-worth. What made matters worse was that the Queensland Government passed the *Aborigines Protection of Alcohol and Opium Act* in 1897. This Act removed abusers of alcohol and drugs to be relocated to reservations, but did not offer any support to overcome their substance-use issues.

- **3rd Generation**: The intergenerational effects of violence manifested in increased physical and emotional spousal abuse, and other forms of domestic violence. Families were also disrupted when *at risk* children were taken from these mothers and placed with non-Indigenous, families.

- **4th Generation**: The original trauma begins to be re-enacted against spouses and children, thus setting the norm of culturally accepted behavior.

- **5th Generation**: The cycle of violence is repeated and compounded, as the unresolved trauma fuels not only more violence, but also is replicated through severity and social distress.

I have discovered that children and adolescents in therapy often describe parents and grandparents who are stuck in their trauma as damaged, preoccupied and emotionally limited. As a result, children struggle to develop a sense of trust, a healthy self-image, social skills and safety in relationships. Traumatized parents also have difficulty with their sense of identity and autonomy, appropriate self-soothing mechanisms and affect regulation, and maintaining a balanced perspective when life challenges arise. In fact, parents often display inappropriate numbed and disassociated responses to everyday stress. Peterson, Joshua, and Feit (2014) also note other issues that include changes in self-perception, such as a chronic and pervasive sense of helplessness, paralysis of initiative, shame, guilt, self-blame, a sense of defilement or stigma, and a sense of being completely different from other human beings. For example, Atkinson (2002) also links historical events associated with the colonization of Aboriginal lands (e.g., 'accidental' epidemics, massacres, starvations, and the removal of people to reserves) to increases in the rates of family violence, child sexual abuse and family breakdown in indigenous society. An ongoing challenge for healing trauma in survivors becomes extremely difficult when entire communities and cultures become stuck in their traumas related to war, genocide, torture, massacre, etc. In these

James A. Houck, Jr., Ph.D.

cases, traditional counseling is hardly effective when everybody is traumatized. In fact, trauma appears to reproduce itself, as long as, the social causes are not addressed, and offenders continue to benefit from exemption for their crimes.

CHAPTER FOUR

If I Only Had a Self:
Transmuting Trauma

Healthy children will not fear life
if their elders have integrity enough not to fear death.

Erik Erkison

Reconnecting

Over the years, although treatment for PTSD has taken on many forms, the desired outcome remained the same: *Reconnection to what was lost.* Of course, personal safety is still the primary concern for the traumatized person, as triggers always have the potential to create unsafe conditions. In fact, a traumatized person may seek professional help in alleviating the above symptoms. However, in conjunction with personal safety is the overall treatment goal of helping the person reconnect with his/her intrapersonal and interpersonal relationships. Reconnecting intrapersonal relationship by examining personal assumptions about a sense of control and power in their lives, as well as healing interpersonal relationships in which issues of trust, safety, self-esteem, etc., may have been shattered. These tasks may be especially difficult if the person has defined themselves been defined by the trauma. Add to this phenomenon that in *intergenerational trauma*, what has been handed down has been not only the traumatic symptoms, but also a distorted view of themselves.

The debate of *how* trauma is transmitted from one relationship to another has dominated the studies of Intergenerational Trauma (IT) for some time. Interestingly, transmission of IT is an on-going conversation generated by people who understand trauma transmission from either a nature or nurture viewpoint. From the *nature* viewpoint, beliefs center on trauma as being contained and handed down through the genes, the DNA from great grandparents to grandparents to parents to children, etc. The *nurture* side of the argument believes that trauma is passed down through the way we are raised; our attachments with caregivers, as well as how we develop throughout our lives. To be honest, both sides present convincing examples of the transmission of trauma, but in the end, it is it is a both/ and understanding. In other words, we may be predisposed to trauma through our family line, our ancestors, but how we are nurtured does affect the degree to which intergenerational trauma can be triggered in us through unresolved trauma in our great grandparents, grandparents, parents, etc.

> *Like silt deposited on the cogs of a finely tuned machine after the seawater of a tsunami recedes, our experiences, and those of our forebears, are never gone, even if they have been forgotten. They become a part of us, a molecular residue holding fast to our genetic scaffolding. The DNA remains the same, but psychological and behavioral tendencies are inherited. You might have inherited not just your grandmother's knobby knees, but also her predisposition toward depression caused by the neglect she suffered as a newborn.*
>
> Hurley (2015)

Epigenetics

Over the past century, epigenetics has played a major role regarding understanding how trauma is passed down from generation to generation to generation. In 2008, a conference at Cold Spring Harbor, NY, epigenetics was defined as *stable, inheritable physical traits that resulted from changes the way genes function.* In layman terms this means that our DNA is responsible for storing and transferring genetic information. However, it is the RNA (Ribonucleic Acid) which provides our DNA *codes* for the production of amino acids, acting as a messenger between DNA and ribosomes to make proteins (Helmenstime, 2015). If not enough proteins are produced, neural connections in the brain are diminished, which affects our moods. *Epigenetics*, originally coined by Waddington (1942), describes this influence (at, on, over, etc.) of genetic processes on brain development. In other words, influences, such as trauma, can alter the functions of RNA and DNA. Moreover, if a person's life was/is greatly affected by traumatic events, these have the potential to make a lasting impressing on one's DNA, or an *epigenetic mark*; an indicator that the gene has been altered by traumatic experiences (Berger, 2009). Therefore, if trauma occurs at a critical period in a person's development, the genetic pattern can be set for the rest of his/her life (Carey, 2012).

In an article entitled, *Can Trauma Be Passed On Through Our DNA?* Davis (2016) states that *the single most dangerous idea I learned in school is that the genes you get from you parents are passed on to your children, and nothing you do in your life changes them.* Many people I talk to also believe that their physical traits and family illnesses cannot be changed. However, challenging this notion, Davis states that although people do indeed pass on the exact same chromosomes from grandparent, parent to child, the *quality* of these chromosomes, when they are received, has the potential to be enhanced or diminished, according to what happens to us and the choices we make during our lifetime. In a way, these studies tap into Pavlov's Theory of Classical Conditioning. Initially, Pavlov was able to *condition* a dog's mouth-watering response to the smell of meat powder, with the ringing of a bell. Each time Pavlov rang the bell, he produced the meat powder, which in turn, made the dog's mouth water. Eventually, the dog learned to associate hearing the bell with food. This initial experiment led Pavlov to further understand how human beings are also conditioned by various experiences. For example, a person who has had a near drowning experience might become conditioned to fear the sound of rushing water, such as the crashing of ocean waves, or the rapid torrent of a river. The sound of such water may conjure up heightened anxiety, hypervigilance, pounding heart rate, sensations of suffocation, tightness in one's chest, etc. While there is an element of safety in fear itself, (especially if the person cannot swim in rushing water) fear becomes another matter altogether when these same physiological reactions are experienced when filling a bathtub with water. The element of danger is reduced, yet the mind and body reacts and shifts into survival mode. Yet, are these self-preservation conditioned responses something we keep to ourselves, or have they been passed on genetically to us from our ancestors?

Conversely, Geddes (2013) notes that is possible for some information to be inherited biologically through chemical changes that occur in our DNA, namely conditioned fears associated with a sense of smell. During controlled tests with mice, researchers learned that mice can pass on conditioned information about traumatic or stressful experiences, such as associating an electrical shock with the smell of a cherry blossom. Interestingly, the study discovered that future generations of mice, whose biological father or grandfather learned to associate the smell of cherry blossom with an electric shock, became jumpier in the presence of the same odor, and responded to lower concentrations of it than normal mice. Subsequently, Dias (2016), from the Department of Psychiatry at Emory University, suggests that such experiences are somehow transferred from the brain into the DNA (like a fingerprint), which not only changes the structure of the chromosome, but also conditions the genes to be passed on to later generations:

> From a translational perspective, our results allow us to appreciate how the experiences of a parent, before even conceiving offspring, markedly influence both structure and function in the nervous system of subsequent generations... Such a phenomenon may contribute to the

etiology and potential intergenerational transmission
of risk for neuropsychiatric disorders such as phobias,
anxiety and post-traumatic stress disorder.

McCraty (2004) writes that the heart, like the brain, generates a powerful electromagnetic field, which can be measured several feet away from a person's body and between two individuals in close proximity. For example, how many times have we walked by someone and felt a certain negative *vibe*, or sitting near people who expressively happy and feel a certain lift in our emotions? I am certain we have experienced this phenomenon. The same is true with us. Without us realizing it, our cardio-electro-magnetic field gives off information when we are angry, fearful, depressed or experiencing some other negative emotion, as well as empathy, compassion, gratitude or love when we experience something positive. In another study from the HeartMath Institute entitled, *The Heart-Brain Synchronization Between Mother and Baby* (2008), studied the energetic heart-brain interactions that occur between a mother and her infant.

Researchers were able to show that the mother's brainwaves synchronized to that of her baby's heartbeat. It appears that when the mother placed her attention on the baby that she became more sensitive to the subtle electromagnetic signals generated by the infant's heart. From these studies, there is strong evidence to suggest that our social interactions have the potential to not only affect family members, but also all relationships. Bernstein (2016) notes that exposures to war, severe stress, death, starvation, disease, etc., that occur prior to conception, and in utero, can have lasting effects on subsequent generations. For example, how trauma can be passed on to future generations through genetics can be supported by experiences during the Dutch Famine of 1944-1945. During World War II, although the Netherlands took a neutral stance in the war, Hitler's troops invaded and took control of the country by May 1940. To avoid capture, the Dutch government and the royal family fled to England. Despite the fact that by September

James A. Houck, Jr., Ph.D.

1944, Allied troops had liberated most of the country in the south, however, their advances towards northern Netherlands were halted at the Waal and Rhine rivers and the Battle of Arnhem. In support of the Allied war effort, the Dutch government in exile in London called for a national railway strike to hinder German military initiatives. In retaliation, in October 1944, the German authorities blocked all food supplies to the occupied West of the country. The *Hongerwinter,* or Hunger Winter, as it has been described, was the time when food supplies became increasingly scarce. For approximately eight months, widespread starvation and infectious diseases of the digestive system, were seen especially in the cities of the western Netherlands (Banning, 1946). Interestingly, such trauma also affected the reproductive outcomes of women who gave birth during this period. These newborns, who were exposed to this famine during gestation, were reported to have lower birth weights, malformations, and increased perinatal mortality. In addition, long-term developmental effects of the famine could be seen in increased physical and psychological effects of infants born during the famine (Lumey and Van Poppel, 1994).

Intergenerational genetic changes resulting from trauma was also studied in the Holocaust survivors and their children at Mount Sinai School of Medicine in New York City. Led by Rachel Yehuda, a neuroscientist and the director of the traumatic stress studies division, studied whether the risk of mental illness resulting from traumatic experiences is biologically passed on from one generation to the next? A sample of 32 Jewish men and women, who had either been captive in Nazi concentration camps, witnessed or experienced physical and/ or emotional torture, or who went into seclusion out of fear of being captured by the Nazis, were part of the study. Their genes, as well as the genes of their children, were compared with the results of Jewish families who lived outside Europe during WWII. In children born to Holocaust survivors, Yehuda discovered an *epigenetic mark,* or a change to the genes that affects the way the DNA is read into RNA, in the children born to Holocaust survivors. In addition, she also notes that these children displayed an increased likelihood of stress disorders (Samuels, 2014).

Epigenetics has also been studied in Native American populations who have suffered historical trauma. Pember (2015) notes that high rates of addiction, suicide, mental illness, sexual violence and other ills among Native Americans can be traced back through epigenetics to a "colonial health deficit," or the result of colonization and its aftermath. According to the American Indian and Alaska Native Genetics Research Guide created by the National Congress of American Indians (NCAI), studies have shown that various behavior and health conditions are due to inherited epigenetic changes. For example, a 2008 study by Moshe Szyf at McGill University in Montreal examined the brains of suicide victims, who were abused as children. Szyf and his team found that genes governing stress responses (e.g., increase in heart rate, rapid shallow breathing, sweating, etc.) in the victim's hippocampus had been methylated or *switched off* (Ibid, 2015). When people experience excessive trauma, the liver produces hormones called glucocorticoids. Once the trauma has past, glucocorticoid levels return to normal. However, if people are exposed to relentless trauma, continuous exposure to this hormone can inhibit genes in the hippocampus' ability to regulate glucocorticoids, thus switching them off, and ultimately affecting our mood. As time goes on, there appears to be more and more research pointing to the significance of epigenetics that explains intergenerational trauma. In commenting on the importance of such studies, Professor Emeritus Marcus Pembrey (2013), a pediatric geneticist at University College London, notes:

> It (epigenetics) addresses constitutional fearfulness
> that is highly relevant to phobias, anxiety and post-
> traumatic stress disorders, plus the controversial subject
> of transmission of the 'memory' of ancestral experience
> down the generations...It is high time public health
> researchers took human transgenerational responses

seriously. I suspect we will not understand the rise in neuropsychiatric disorders or obesity, diabetes and metabolic disruptions generally without taking a multigenerational approach.

Furthermore, as awareness of epigenetics grows, it will shed light on the quality of our own genes, not only for the betterment of generations yet to be born, but also empowers us to heal our own intergenerational traumas.

Nurture

When considering intergenerational trauma, it is important also to include relational and environmental factors that mold and shape who we are. Although the *nature* side of this debate refers to the genetic makeup inherited from biological great-grandparents to grandparents to parent to child, etc., the *nurture* side refers to the development of the *intrapersonal* (what occurs within the self) and *interpersonal* (what occurs between two or more people) relationships throughout our lives. This development also extends toward our environment and involves the process of learning through our daily experiences. These two factors of human relationships and the environment eventually culminated in the study of Developmental Psychology. Developmental Psychology emerged as a psycho-social discipline in the post-industrial revolution, striving to produce a more educated workforce, as well as to produce a more effective education and learning environments for children. Developmental Psychology, also known as Human Development, focuses on human growth and changes across the lifespan from conception to death. This discipline also focuses on the physical, cognitive, social, intellectual, perceptual, personality and emotional growth; a continual and cumulative process. Basically, the strength of human development I believe lies in its focus on addressing our growth across the life span.

This focus also empowers us to embrace our capacity to contribute to our own psychological development, i.e., integrate, conceptualize, and organize our own experiences in order to direct our lives. It also encompasses our social development, namely our ethnic identity, norms, customs, etc. (Newman and Newman, 2014).

Erik Erikson (1994) was perhaps most known for his theory on psychosocial development. Throughout his life, Erikson emphasized how humanity develops a healthy sense of ourselves, while at the same time, resolves any internal conflicts that emerge as we integrate roles and/or expectations of culture and society. For example, Erikson developed an eight-stage progression that tracks growth and development throughout the lifespan:

- Trust vs. Mistrust (birth to age two): Erikson believed that an infant whose basic needs are met, i.e., food, comfort, diaper changes, etc., will develop a sense of trust in others, as well as a sense of trustworthiness in himself/herself. If a child's basic needs are not met, the child will develop a sense of mistrust of having others meet his/her needs, become frustrated, withdrawn, suspicious, and will lack self-confidence.
- Autonomy vs. Shame & Doubt (age two to age four): Caregivers provide affirmation, support, and exploration of the home, whereby a child can develop a sense of self-control and self-esteem, such as mastering toilet training. If the caregivers do not provide such affirmation, support and exploration of the home, etc., a child may experience shame and doubt about his/her self-control and independence.
- Initiative vs. Guilt (ages four to six): The child develops a sense of responsibility and accomplishment, such as learning to dress himself/herself, which increases initiative to attempt new things during this period. If the child is made to feel irresponsible and anxious about not being able to do certain things, they will have uncomfortable guilt feelings, and thereby not likely to attempt new things.

- Industry vs. Inferiority (age six to puberty): The child develops a sense of discovery, acquiring knowledge and work, namely through school and a widening circle of friends. However, learning does not exclusively occur in the classroom, but also at home, with friends who teach teamwork namely through sports or other group activities. Erikson believed that successful experiences at this stage gives the child a sense of feeling competence and mastery, while disappointment gives them a sense of inadequacy and inferiority to others.

- Identity vs. Identity confusion (adolescence): During this period, teenagers seek out their true selves. Erikson believed this is the time when adolescents commit to a particular identity, handle peer pressure, and begin to realize things about themselves that will play a role in shaping their futures. If adolescents are unable to accomplish these aspects, uncertainty and confusion slows this process.

- Intimacy vs. Isolation (ages 22 to 35 years): Young adults focus on forming intimate, loving relationships with other people. Issues of dating, marriage, remaining single, beginning families, and career choices are all characteristic of this stage.

- Generativity vs. Stagnation (ages 35 to 66 years): Middle adulthood is characterized by the need to create or nurture things that will outlast the individual, namely raising a family, working, and contributing to the community, are all ways that people develop a sense of purpose. When the individual feels that he has done nothing to help the next generation then they may experience a sense of stagnation, feeling disconnected from others and useless.

- Integrity vs. Despair (ages 60 to 75 years): This is the time in which people look back on their life with a sense of integrity, acceptance and accomplishment, or with a sense of despair, regret and hopelessness.

A ninth stage was added later.

- Immortality verses Extinction (Ages 75 to death): At this stage, people are coping with an emotional, physical, psychological and spiritual *life review.* Storytelling and an assurance about meaningfulness of life and key features of this stage. As people are faced with their mortality and the physical/mental changes with aging, they can either accept death with a sense of integrity and without fear, or struggle with letting go of losses that preceded death.

Attachment Theory

One of the aspects that make human beings unique is our capacity to emotionally, physically and spiritually bond with people, animals, and places. Most of the time we take these relationships for granted, however, these bonds affect everything that we do from family, friends, education, and careers, to recreation, spirituality and caring for other generations. Depending on the strength of these bonds, we also discover how we form relational trusts in striving for new adventures or new tasks in our life, such as willing to explore new experiences, cultivate sexual intimacy, give back to others, develop a sense of identity, even how we maintain these bonds in the light of our physical mortality.

Key figures in the study of relational attachment are Mary Ainsworth (1913-1999) and John Bowlby (1907-1990). Ainsworth (1970) is perhaps most remembered for developing the *Strange Situation,* which studied the reaction between the bonding attachments between toddlers and their mothers. Ainsworth hypothesized that any child who is threatened or stressed in relationships will naturally move toward caregivers who create a sense of physical, emotional and psychological safety for them. For example, from behind a two-way mirror, Ainsworth watched the reaction of toddlers when their mothers left the room and a stranger appeared. The reactions were fascinating. For some children, when they noticed that their mothers had left the room, did not display any concern, but initiated play with the stranger. In another instance when the mother left the room, the child seemed quite anxious and looked for his/her mother nervously, while basically ignoring the stranger. In yet another example, when the mother left the room, the child had a complete emotional meltdown and was in so much distress, that he/she became immobilized. Not even the stranger could console them. To complete the experiment, Ainsworth noted the toddler's reaction when his/her mother returned to the room. For the child who noticed that mom was missing, yet continued to play with the stranger, acknowledged mom's return, and went back to playing. For the child who was anxious and distressed when mom left the room, he/she became very emotional and clingy to mom upon her return. This child needed much comfort, soothing, and reassurance from the mother. For the child who had the meltdown, he/she was inconsolable, and was quite angry with mom for leaving in the first place.

Through replicating these experiments, Ainsworth developed her theory on different types of human attachment, which not only applied to how relational trust begins early on in life, but also displays patterns of how we form attachments throughout our lives, namely, *Secure Attachment, Anxious Avoidant Attachment, Anxious Resistant Attachment and Disorganized Disoriented Attachment* (Ainsworth, Blehar, Waters and Wall, 2015). An example of secure attachment continuing in adulthood would be when people feel confident in who they are, and is able to meet their own needs. This person often enjoys open, physical and emotional intimate, meaningful relationships. On the other hand, if people were raised without the nurturing and attention of a regular caregiver, or perhaps they suffered extreme abuse or neglect, then adult relationships will more than likely be characterized by aggression, clinging behavior, emotional detachment, psychosomatic and/or mood disorders, etc. (Ibid, 2015).

Attachment Theory provides a model not only to conceptualize the tendency in human beings to make strong affective bonds with others, but also to understand the strong emotional and physiological reactions that occur when those bonds are perceived to have been broken (Bowlby, 1982). For example, any change in the attachment, e.g. emotional or physical separation, creates a loss (real or perceived), and in turn, produces grief. The more secure emotional attachment a person has toward a loved one, the greater a person's ability to adapt to changes in his/her social functioning following the loved one's death. The ability to adapt to a loved one's death is mainly due in part to emotionally and spiritually holding that loved one in another place in our lives, which then enables us to form new attachments (Houck, 2010). We are able to do this because although death ends a physical bond, it can never end the emotional and spiritual bonds that we have with the loved one. In other words, the relationship is always there.

For people who have anxious resistant or anxious avoidant attachment styles, they may be more likely to be concerned over *who is going to take care of me now*, or *I don't know I can go on without _____ in my life?* Furthermore, for people who have developed a disorganized disoriented attachment (often being diagnosed with reactive attachment disorder in childhood) have very stormy, co-dependent and sometimes, violent relationships. Such people will more than likely have the hardest time coming to terms with his/her feelings of loss and grief. In fact, although the emotional and spiritual connection remains with the deceased loved one, survivors will often interpret their death as feeling abandoned, and will display anger/rage, resentment, bitterness, and thereby making forming new attachments extremely difficult.

Vygotsky's Zone of Proximal Development

Lev Vygotsky (1896-1934) was a Russian psychologist, who believed that children attained more sophisticated reasoning skills through interaction with their social, cultural world. Again, similar to attachment theory, the more *hands on experience* children have with people in their society, the more they could learn new tasks. Vygotsky (1978) coined the phrase *zone of proximal development* which referred to the time when children are *apprentices* in need of adults, or masters, to teach and demonstrate them how to attain and apply knowledge of their environment. This kind of learning is also reinforced when children learn from their peers. This technique is called *scaffolding* because it builds upon knowledge children already have with new knowledge that adults can help the child learn (Wood et al, 1976). Once the student, with the benefit of scaffolding, masters a task, the scaffolding can then be removed, and the student will then be able to complete the task again on his own. *Differentiation* is another educational strategy in which students of different abilities, learning needs, and levels of academic achievement are grouped together (Abbot, 2014). The overall goal for all students is to master essential knowledge, concepts, and skills, but teachers may use different instructional methods (e.g., cultural applications) to help students meet those expectations.

We often see Vygotsky's theory at work in the world of coaching and sports. All in all, the player goes from novice, to apprentice, to seasoned player. In fact, a child who begins sports early in life, like say, baseball, will need to master the fundamentals, e.g., batting, catching, throwing, sliding. This is one level of learning. As the child matures and wants to continue playing baseball, even dreams of one day pitching in minor and major leagues, the player will often work with pitching coaches who constantly evaluate the pitcher's ball velocity, gripping the ball, throwing fast balls, sliders, curve balls, change ups, communicating with catchers, body contortion, muscle conditioning, etc. All these evaluations are to help the pitcher develop and integrate these skills, are part of scaffolding. Initially, learning basic techniques may appear to be mechanical and stiff, but once the pitcher has mastered these skills, they are integrated into a more fluid execution of pitching. These same processes are true in anything we do. Initially, we approach everything in life with a limited knowledge and skill. However, we are taught the *how, when, where,* and *why* we do things, from the hands of those who are more experienced. As a result, we build upon the knowledge and skills the more we integrate them in our lives.

All in all, the nature/nurture debate continues to this day. Although there are well sounding perspectives on both sides, it is clear that intergenerational trauma disrupts and distorts our biological, psychological and social development. Whether intergenerational trauma is passed onto succeeding generations through altered genes, dysfunctional emotional attachments and/or inappropriate learned behaviors, one thing is certain: intergenerational trauma distorts the true sense of who we are as souls. In fact, once we fully embrace this soul consciousness, we are then empowered to see ourselves for who we are, not merely as by-products of our upbringing and environment.

The Under Developed Self:

In his work, *The Analysis of the Self* (1971), psychologist Heinz Kohut defines the self as a person's psychological being, which consists of sensations, feelings, thoughts, and attitudes toward oneself and the world. According to his model of *Self-Psychology,* Kohut understood our inability to overcome many issues in our lives as stemming from an underdeveloped sense of who we are. Moreover, not only are we simply not aware of who we are, but also, we are not aware of what inner gifts, beauty and strengths we possess; external *objects* in our lives have been substituted for what we really desire in relationships, e.g., love, acceptance, peace, intimacy, nurturing, courage, etc. For example, in order to develop a healthy self, we are required to *internalize the qualities* of external objects in our lives. If we grew up with a favorite stuffed animal or toy, we learned the value of comfort, fun and companionship, etc., that the toy provided. The reason such external objects connect with us is because they meet an inner emotional and psychological need. However, although this is normal behavior in childhood, as we mature, we internalize these qualities, and now substitute the stuffed animal/toy for more meaningful, emotional, physical and sexual intimacy in relationships with others. If we are unable to do this, we will struggle to reciprocate these human qualities in meaningful, life-giving ways. A more contemporary example of this struggle people face in moving from an underdeveloped sense of self, toward a healthy self, comes from the movie *Ted* (Fantasy/Buddy film, 2012). In this film, John Bennett, a 35-year-old man-child received his childhood wish in making his teddy bear (Ted) come to life. Growing up, Ted served as a great companion, confidant and unconditional love for John. Unfortunately, John never internalized these *qualities* he received from Ted (object), and thus struggled to find meaning in his relationships, namely his girlfriend Lori, without Ted always being around.

Many people also look at external objects in order to satisfy the inner stirrings of the soul. Whether they are objects that provide pleasure, happiness, comfort, security and/or peace, they can never touch the cry of the soul consciousness that connects us with God. These objects are simply poor substitutes that on one level, serve to meet our emotional and/or physical needs. However, the reason why we cling to external objects is because, on one level, they work. For example, alcohol is a depressant and calms emotional anxiety and stress. Cocaine is a stimulant and boosts mental and physical energy. Sexual orgasms releases dopamine in the brain and provides a physiological sense of elation, and a lengthy work out releases endorphins and provides us with an analgesic feeling. Yet on the other hand, if we truly want to understand ourselves as soul, we must learn that these external objects always point us to connect with a higher consciousness that transcends our emotional, psychological and physical realms. In fact, as we listen to the cry of our soul, we realize our deepest desire is to connect/reconnect to the purest sense of who we are. In fact, this cry of our soul is so powerful, so deafening, that once we fully embrace ourselves, we will never be satisfied with anything less.

Intergenerational Trauma Disrupts the Self

As stated earlier, trauma has the potential to disconnect us from who we are as soul. The reason for this is because trauma places a distorted template over our perceptions. Trauma says to us: *This is all there is. This is all there is to you.. This is as good as it gets.* All lies and distortions that come from other wounded people who have yet to embrace themselves as soul. In fact, once we embrace ourselves as soul, we may be astonished to see the power of our soul to not only transcend trauma and transform our wounded energy, but also empower others to do the same. Still, as history teaches us, many have feared the resiliency and power of the soul, and therefore, have tried to silence its cry. Through killings, murders, genocide, starvations, forced assimilations, humiliations, degradations, looking at people as savages, primitive, backward, unworthy, unlovable, and therefore, disposable as those in control see fit. What is heart breaking to me is that these atrocities have often been committed in the name of God, by people who *should* see themselves as soul. In fact, even when killing is done in the name of advancing the Kingdom of God, the only thing that is truly advanced is the distorted view from those who will do anything to hang on to their power. Moreover, Jesus warned those in his day who claimed to *know* God, but treated others with contempt:

> *But woe to you, scribes and Pharisees, hypocrites!*
> *For you shut the kingdom of heaven in people's faces.*
> *For you neither enter yourselves nor allow those who*
> *would enter to go in. Woe to you, scribes and Pharisees,*
> *hypocrites! For you travel across sea and land to make*
> *a single proselyte, and when he becomes a proselyte, you*
> *make him twice as much a child of hell as yourselves...Woe*
> *to you, scribes and Pharisees, hypocrites! For you are*
> *like white-washed tombs, which outwardly appear*
> *beautiful, but within are full of dead people's bones*
> *and all uncleanness. So you also outwardly appear*

*righteous to others, but within you are full of hypocrisy
and lawlessness. Woe to you, scribes and Pharisees,
hypocrites! For you build the tombs of the prophets
and decorate the monuments of the righteous, saying,
'If we had lived in the days of our fathers, we would
not have taken part with them in shedding the blood of
the prophets.' Thus you witness against yourselves that
you are sons of those who murdered the prophets. Fill
up, then, the measure of your fathers. You serpents, you
brood of vipers, how are you to escape being sentenced
to hell? Therefore, I send you prophets and wise men
and scribes, some of whom you will kill and crucify,
and some you will flog in your synagogues and persecute
from town to town, so that on you may come all the
righteous blood shed on earth, from the blood of
righteous Abel to the blood of Zechariah the son of
Barachiah, whom you murdered between the sanctuary
and the altar.*

Matthew 23:13-35

Trauma is not the only thing that has been passed down through
the generations, but also it is the very systems that fuel prejudices,
feelings of contempt, and a distorted view of life that have been
galvanized, or reinforced, that often leaves generations in voiceless
disparity. However, a huge part of healing intergenerational trauma,
and moving people toward a healthy sense of self, involves not only
understanding these historical distortions, but also grieving that
which has been taken from them. For example, I explain this process
in counseling therapy as being similar to the movie *The Wizard of
Oz*. The storyline involves powerful lessons because most people
can typically relate to this movie on some personal level. Perhaps
one reason why this movie is such a beloved classic is that there are
two stories going on at the same time: On one hand, we are taken
on a journey with the companions of Dorothy; the scarecrow, the

cowardly lion, and the tin man. They all are in search of something they believe is *lacking* in them, so their adventures take them to seek the Wizard. The tin man needed a heart. The scarecrow needed a brain. The cowardly lion needed courage, and of course, Dorothy wanted to go home. Yet on the other hand, this trip is really about an *inward journey* they make in order to discover who they are. As they set out, their journey is filled with dangerous encounters and harrowing escapes from the Wicked Witch of the West and her minions. After the Witch was defeated, as the Wizard commanded, and all was well, the four companions go back to the Wizard to receive their rewards. The Wizard then takes them back in time and explains that through their ordeal, they each displayed what they lacked. The tin man displayed a tremendous heart of devotion and loyalty. The scarecrow turned out to be the *brains* of the outfit. The cowardly lion showed remarkable courage in the face of overwhelming odds, and Dorothy, as we all know, had the ability to go home anytime she wanted. She finally realized that there was no other place more magical than her own home and those who loved her. In the story of the Wizard of Oz, we have a classic example of people who are in search of things that they believe they lack, but later come to realize, that they had these characteristics all along.

I have yet to meet anyone who begins a journey of self-discovery that sooner or later, must work through personal and family traumatic experiences, as well as re-examine stories that have been handed down to them by those *also* needing to come to terms with their own trauma. In this sense, family perspectives and interpretations of traumatic events seem to go hand in hand. In fact, sometimes trauma becomes a way in which individuals, families and generations have defined themselves, which internally perpetuates the cycle of intergenerational trauma. For example, if grandparents, parents and other caregivers do not have a healthy sense of themselves, or they too are struggling with intergenerational traumatic experiences, they will unconsciously pass their issues on to younger generations in terms of their fears, anxieties, insecurities, and abandonment, to name a few.

Affect regulation is a skill that develops quite early in us, as we gauge how others mirror their emotions appropriately or inappropriately. Although as newborns we were unable, at that time, to form words, we were able to form mental and emotional perceptions from how we were held and spoken to. In fact, we were so skilled at this that we could tell when our caregivers were holding us verses when we were being held by a stranger. For example, we picked up on facial expressions; eyebrows raised and a smile indicating love and acceptance, or if we see a furled brow and frown, we interpret that expression as something being wrong. In the *Still Face Experiment,* developmental psychologist Edward Tronick (1975) concluded that an infant develops reciprocal patterns of expressions when interacting with his/her mother. For example, when the mother engages her infant with smiles, laughter and other positive facial expressions, the infant mimics these cues. However, when the mother's face is expressionless and unresponsive, the infant notices this change immediately. As a result, the infant makes repeated attempts to get the interaction back to its previous reciprocal pattern. All in all, Tronick's study supported the fact that at this early stage, our senses are so in tuned with *reading* others and the world around us, that our self-identity begins to take shape and continues throughout our lives (Adamson and Frick, 2003). Just imagine the potential to create a healthy sense of self in children, when caregivers nurture from a place of the soul!

The Soulful Wisdom of Indigenous Grandmothers

There is an ancient tradition among indigenous tribes which involves a powerful blessing from the grandmothers when a baby is born. Before the newborn is returned to the mother, the grandmothers of the village would take turns holding the child. Looking deep into his/her eyes and with a loving tone, the grandmothers would speak words of affirmation and tell the child how much he/she is loved by this community, loved by God, and is gifted with many good and precious gifts as a beautiful soul. This grandmothers' tradition begins the internalization process of love, security and trust in the infant, and truly reinforces the idea that it indeed takes a village to raise a child.

There is a beauty to counseling therapy that is not just about alleviating mental health symptoms troubling clients. It also involves helping people discover who they are, and the gifts and character strengths they have. In other words, helping people remove their emotional, behavioral and/or spiritual obstructions, so that they may embrace their authentic selves. In the book, *Reclaiming Authenticity* (Houck, 2014), I state that everyone has been given what they need when they come into this world; their power, energy, gifts, talents, resiliencies, etc. However, it is through various experiences that we are often misled to believe that in order to survive or thrive, we must first deny who we are, give away our power and settle for living by another's inauthentic definition and rules. As a result, we end up searching for our true selves in all the wrong places, instead of looking within our own soul. Interestingly, when people fully embrace the fact that they are a soul, and are indeed precious in the eyes of God, the compassionate, nurturing side of humanity emerges in a powerful way. Issues of prejudice, sexism, egocentrism, racism, etc. all go out the window; these simply cannot dwell in the higher consciousness of the soul.

Helping generations heal from traumatic issues in which they had learned mistrust, or internalized skewed perceptions which affected their attachments, cognitive development and social interactions, has a multidimensional and mutigenerational effect. When generations of a family are able to come together and address these issues, they quickly realize that healing such wounds is not a matter of placing blame, but instead, understanding the impact of what has been handed down through the generations. Yes, there is a level of accountability and restorative justice that also needs to be addressed, but more importantly acknowledge perhaps the woundedness that has been passed on from many generations before. People who have been wounded, wound others. For example, if a family member is struggling with an addiction, chances are that there is a family system in place that reinforces that wound. Going back through the generation then, family members might become aware of how many others had addiction issues. Suicide is also another family dynamic that comes down through generations. Families are certainly wise to investigate how certain emotional, psychological, sociological, etc., factors set the stage for such perceptions and behaviors to unfold. Even if suicide attempts have not occurred in the present generation, feelings of hopelessness and despair may have infiltrated a family's perceptions of powerlessness.

For the most part, healing is a matter of unlearning these generational lessons that have affected what family members have believed about themselves, as well as how these perceptions have affected their behaviors toward one another (Sandwell, 2008). Even if one's parents and grandparents are deceased, healing can still be achieved by understanding the dynamics of trauma that has been handed down in the family, as well as appreciating the resiliency and other character strengths family members possess. Emotional and psychological wounds are not the only thing that we may have inherited; our character strengths, gifts and skills also were handed down.

CHAPTER FIVE

Non-Apologies Become the
Salt in Tomorrow's Tears

An apology has three parts:
I'm sorry.
It is my fault.
What can I do to make it right?

Anonymous

The Sting of Public Apologies

Another aspect of intergenerational trauma that seems to go hand in hand with the soul's inability to move on is the public apology. Within recent decades, there has been a steady stream of public apologies made on behalf of government and ecclesiastical leaders, for the inhumane treatment, sexual abuses, prejudiced behavior and outright slaughter of people from many cultural backgrounds. The public acknowledgement of such behavior comes often as a result of uncovering crimes against humanity, investigative reporting, and/or the work of truth commissions, to name a few. Albeit a step in the right direction, some of these public apologies for historical atrocities, often include an air of dismissive justification of *that's the way the world was back then* explanation for the mistreatment of people for the greater good of a nation or world. In a sense, contemporary leaders often offer an apology for the past, without accepting responsibility for doing anything wrong, let alone not acknowledging being part of socio-economic, political, educational and/or religious systems that still perpetuate oppressive schemes. Whether it was the advancement of science, manifest destiny or believed to be a divine right, violence, in one form or another has always been justified against a weaker, under-educated, under-civilized, and/or under-developed people (Black, 2012). Ironically, this rational for force always seems to come from the perspectives of people who use their military might, political power, religious zeal, and/or outright lust to hang onto their piece of power and control for as long as possible. In fact, history often bears witness to this phenomenon from generation to generation to generation. Repeatedly, physical, emotional, psychological and spiritual abuses incriminate those who have exploited and manipulated their power for either world-wide colonization, and/or genocide in countries such as America, Canada, The Congo, Germany, Russia, Rwanda, Ireland, Australia, and in fact, anywhere else violence and genocide have occurred.

On one hand, public apologies do acknowledge the cruel and inhumane acts done to vulnerable populations. Such apologies raise a sense of community awareness and empathy regarding the devastating and intergenerational traumatic effects of the suffering of others. As words of empathy are offered, many victims and survivors feel vindicated and are grateful for the public voices raised on behalf of those who have yet to find their healing voice. On the other hand, some public apologies are very superficial, and are often rejected by contemporary populations whose ancestors have not only been victimized in such horrors, but succeeding generations continue to feel that accountability and justice has never really been served. For many, apologies, explanations and the offer of financial compensation, only add insult to intergenerational wounds in people, who continue to feel the sting of a hand slapped across the face. For example, McEvers (2015) recalls a speech made on July 10, 2015, that Pope Francis apologized to Bolivia's indigenous leaders for the Church's crimes and sins against native people: *I would also say, and here I wish to be quite clear, as was St. John Paul II: I humbly ask forgiveness, not only for the offenses of the church herself, but also for crimes committed against the native peoples during the so-called conquest of America.*

Although his apology initially was warmly received, many California Native American Indian populations felt betrayed when Pope Francis, within two months of this apology, canonized Fr. Junipero Serra in Washington, DC. Despite the fact that he established nine of the 21 missions along the California coast in the 1700's, Fr. Serra has been widely criticized over his physical mistreatment and suppression of native peoples. Moreover, whereas once hundreds of thousands of California Native American Indians flourished, within 100 years of Fr. Serra's arrival, the indigenous population had been decimated to 16,000 (Houska, 2015).

Perhaps another reason why public apologies often fall short in their effectiveness to bring healing, is because of the confusing motivation behind the apology. Are public apologies meant to excuse behavior, or dismiss accountability? Are public apologies able to capture the historical perspective that justifies behavior based on what was considered legal at the time, or do public apologies simply point out the ethical/moral injustices? From the benefit of hindsight, we might interpret that certain actions were unethical/immoral in their day, but nonetheless, were permitted because people acted according to the *legem terrae,* or law of the land. In other words, are public apologies now considered appropriate based on actions that were considered legal according to our contemporary laws or the laws of those times? For example, in an October 2014 Tuam Herald Viewpoint headlined *The Harsh Facts of Life in 1946 Put Modern Controversies in a Different Perspective,* author Joe Coy cautioned readers that *we cannot judge the actions of the past by today's standards... any assessment of those years has to take into account the grinding poverty and lack of resources of the time.* His article was in response to the controversy surrounding the discovery of 796 infants and children buried in an unmarked mass grave in the septic tanks behind the St. Mary's Mother and Baby Home in Tuam County Galway, Ireland. In response, many people still believe that regardless of the economic times, mother/baby homes like that in Tuam and others, were not as affected by the poverty, nor lacked resources as one would think.

In fact, most of the domesticated work such as cooking, tending vegetable gardens, childrearing, etc., were performed by the young mothers who stayed in the Home up to a year after giving birth (Letter to the Editor, *Tuam Herald*, 16th October 2014).

Still, regardless of whether we judge the past according to the present or vice versa, how do the issues of accountability need to be addressed? If public apologies for past atrocities are simply about matters of justice, then why were injustices not addressed at the time in history they were committed? Why now? After all, many of these atrocities have been committed many decades and centuries ago, and the people who took part in such crimes against humanity are deceased, elderly or infirmed. Perhaps the answers lie in the fact that society had a bigger role to play in reinforcing the wishes of a leader or group. Perhaps the systems in place had more to gain than what was considered lost. When I was in Ireland interviewing survivors of these Magdalene Laundries, many women explained to me that how systems kept the *mad, sad,* and the *bad* girls out of sight and in a secret place. They felt betrayed by their families when they were sent to these *Laundries,* often carrying the shame of their *promiscuous* behavior with them. They were made to wear uniforms and work long hours of heavy physical labor. If the girls/women managed to escape, townsfolk identified them by their uniforms, and promptly returned to the *Laundry.* Finally, I asked, *where were the men when all of this was going on?* Interestingly, none of the men were ever punished or shamed like this. In fact, men are hardly ever mentioned at all. Several women shared with me that sometimes it did not matter if you had a boyfriend or not; your shame was a result of emotional, physical and/or sexual abuse by your brother, father, uncle or priest.

In our search for truth and justice, are we content to single out one person as a scapegoat for atrocities, or perhaps are we afraid to admit that such crimes had enough community support and oxygen to be fueled for centuries? Were these atrocities merely a breakdown in the system, or was the system itself faulty to begin with? Furthermore, do we, living in the 21st century, have the resolve to hold our contemporary systems accountable for perpetuating crimes against humanity, regardless of the way things have always been done in the past? Still, a common phrase that drives such inquiries is…*what did they know, and when did they know it?* Regardless of the historical context in which such horrors occurred, it appears that surrounding communities were aware of these atrocities, and passively gave their consent by their silent indifference. Clearly, no one person or group ever involved in crimes against humanity has ever acted alone. In 2015 the movie *Spotlight*, tells the true story of the Boston Globe's uncovering of the child molestation scandal and cover-up within the local Catholic Archdiocese. In one scene, investigator Mitchell Garabedian acknowledges the real issue behind the scandal as he says: *This city, these people... making the rest of us feel like we don't belong. But they're no better than us. Look at how they treat their children. Mark my words, Mr. Rezendes. If it takes a village to raise a child, it takes a village to abuse one.* When it was all said and done, 249 priests and brothers were publicly accused of sexual abuse within the Boston Archdiocese; over 600 stories were published about the scandal. In December 2002, Cardinal Law resigned from the Boston Archdiocese. He was reassigned to the Basilica di Santa Maria Maggiore in Rome, one of the highest ranking Roman Catholic churches in the world.

Family, government, religious, financial, education and socio-economic systems often form a *spider web* of deceitfulness. Just like a spider, the corruption of systems know all too well which threads of the web would allow them to move freely, and which threads would ensnare a population's prey. For example, as previously stated, I interviewed several women who had survived experiences of neglect, abuse and pain at the *Mother/Children Homes* and *Magdalene Laundries*. As I listened to their stories and eye-witness accounts, I could not help wondering what effects these experiences have on a person's soul, let alone the soul of the community? When does reconciliation begin for these women? When they were allowed to leave the *Homes* and *Laundries,* were the women welcomed back into their families and communities who knew where they had been? How do individuals and communities heal from such history now that these institutions no longer exist? Is the horror of the past finally over?

When the *Report of the Commission to Inquire into Child Abuse*, also known as the Ryan Report, was published on May 20, 2009, nobody could have anticipated the public response to the research findings of widespread physical, emotional and sexual abuse of society's most vulnerable, i.e., infants, girls, boys and women in the Irish Residential Institutions. The Executive Team provided a summary in their 2,600-page Report as follows:

- Physical and emotional abuse, as well as and physical and emotional neglect, were prominent features of the institutions.
- Sexual abuse occurred in institutions, and this was particularly as so in boys' institutions.
- Schools were run in a harsh and regimented manner that served to impose unreasonable and oppressive discipline on children and staff alike.
- Children frequently went hungry. At its best the food was inadequate, and it was inedible and badly prepared in many of the schools.
- Many witnesses testified to having been constantly fearful – even terrified – and that these feelings impacted on every aspect of their lives in the institution.
- Prolonged and excessive beatings with implements intended to cause maximum pain occurred with the knowledge and complicity of senior staffers.
- Children were subjected to constant criticism, and verbal abuse. Many were told that they were worthless.
- Some children lost all sense of their identity and kinship, never fully recovering from that loss.

- When children who ran away were caught, they were severely beaten, at times publicly. Some had their heads shaved, and were humiliated in other ways.
- Inspectors, on far-too-rare visits, rarely – if at all – spoke with the children in the institutions.

However, the interviewing team received a more palpable, unedited, account of survivors' atrocities as printed in *Volume V of the Report of the Commission to Inquire into Child Abuse*:

- *Severe physical and sexual abuse.*
- *Stripped naked by a nun and beaten with a stick and given no supper and humiliated.*
- *After running away having my hair cut off to a very short length and was made to stand naked to be beaten by nun in front of other people.*
- *At 6 I was raped by nun and at 10 I was hit with a poker on head by nun.*
- *When I told nuns about being molested by ambulance driver, I was stripped naked and whipped by four nuns to "get the devil out of you".*
- *Sexual and physical abuse, no education, and not enough food.*
- *Forced oral sex and beatings.*
- *A brother tried to rape me but did not succeed, so I was beaten instead.*
- *Taken from bed and made to walk around naked with other boys whilst brothers used their canes and flicked at their penis.*
- *Tied to a cross and raped whilst others masturbated at the side.*
- *I was polishing the floor and a nun placed her foot on my back so I was pushed to the floor. I was locked in a dark room.*
- *Having to empty the toilets and being lifted off the ground by my sideburns.*
- *Put in bath of Jeyes fluid with three others.*

- *Having my head submerged in dirty water in the laundry repeatedly by a nun.*
- *Being beaten regularly*
- *Physical abuse and segregation from other children for no reason.*
- *A severe beating by two nuns for a trivial misdemeanor until I was bleeding.*

On one hand, many people breathed a sigh of relief that finally the stories of thousands of women and children, who had been abused in various ways over the past 60 years, were becoming known. Others were outraged as the Report also exposed the decades of collusion that existed between the Irish government and Catholic organizations who ran these institutions. Previously, the government officials had emphatically stated that these institutions were privately owned and operated by vowed religious people, and therefore, denied any involvement in the mistreatment of the adults, children and babies. However, as far back as the 1940's, the Report highlighted how government inspectors of the *Magdalene Laundries*, did nothing to intervene when they confirmed suspicious reports of broken bones, malnourishment and neglect, as a result of random physical beatings, sexual assault and emotional humiliation of the girls who were forced to live there. Still, many people believed that justice for the victims and survivors would now finally be served, as government (Martin McAleese, Enda Kenny, etc.) and ecclesiastical leaders (Cardinal Sean Brady, Most Reverend Vincent Nichols, etc.) called for accountability and prosecution for anyone responsible for such abuses. However, the survivors' hopes were dashed when it was communicated that the findings would not be used for criminal prosecutions, mainly due to the successful litigation by the *Christian Brothers* to keep the identities of all of its members unnamed in the Report. In fact, *no real names, whether of victims or perpetrators, appear in the final document* (McDonald, 2013).

However, it was not until four years later that the government publicly admitted its role in the mistreatment of thousands of women and girls in the notorious *Magdalene Laundry* system but stopped short of issuing a formal apology (McDonald, 2013). Despite the acknowledgement from Senator Martin McAleese, stating that there was *significant state involvement in how the laundries were run*, Irish Premier Enda Kenny's *regret about the stigma hanging over the women*, and Cardinal Brady *being profoundly sorry and deeply ashamed that children suffered in such awful ways in these institutions*...many survivors felt betrayed by their leaders. In fact, survivors did not think that such public apologies ever touched the depth of their physical, emotional, psychological and spiritual trauma that still plagued them. When the Report also suggested building a permanent memorial, providing counselling and education to survivors, and to improving current child protection services, many people I interviewed interpreted these reparations as suspect. In fact, survivors who were initially filled with elation over the public apology from Taoiseach Enda Kenny, survivors felt because he did not follow through with the recommendations (e.g., *Health Amendment Act of 1996* card for medical care). Therefore, his apology was nothing more than drama (Pollak, 2015).

Over time, government and church officials believed public confidence would be restored and things would get better. Not quite. In 2015, an article entitled *Thousands of Children in Irish Care Homes at Centre of 'Baby Graves Scandal' Were Used in Secret Vaccine Trials in the 1930s,* reported that scientists from the pharmaceutical company, *Burroughs Wellcome,* were involved in secret, illegal vaccine trials for diphtheria on more than 2,000 children in mother-children homes throughout Ireland (Arkell and Neil, 2015). The story detailed that there was no evidence that consent was ever sought, nor any records of how many babies may have died, or suffered debilitating side-effects, as a result. In another story, *Ten Mother and Baby Homes Carried Out Vaccine Trials on Almost 300 Children,* Christina Finn reported that between 1960-1976, Glaxo Smith-Kline conducted similar drug trials on children. The purpose of this trial was to look at the response of the children to a *4-in-1 vaccine,* namely, diphtheria, whooping cough, tetanus, and polio. Again, the State, nor the pharmaceutical company, could not provide any evidence that consent was ever sought, nor any records of how many children died or suffered debilitating side-effects as a result. In addition, the religious orders who ran the homes involved in the trials have also denied that they authorized any clinical trials. Moreover, the mothers of these children also denied such consent (Ó Fátharta, 2014). With the mounting evidence accumulating against government and ecclesiastical systems in Ireland, the old saying is being kept alive in present generations: *The more things change, the more they stay the same.*

The Tuskegee Syphilis Study

The *Tuskegee Study of Untreated Syphilis in the Negro Male* was a clinical study conducted between 1932 and 1972 by the *U.S. Public Health Service*. This study looked at the natural progression of untreated syphilis in rural African-American men in Alabama. These men were told they were receiving free healthcare from the government, but not told about the whole purpose of the study, as well as the dangers involved. Even when Penicillin became the known cure for syphilis in 1947, the Tuskegee men were not being treated appropriately (Jones, 1981). Overall, the victims of the study did not just include African American men who died from syphilis, but also 40 wives who contracted the disease, and 19 of their children were born with congenital syphilis. Overall, the investigation identified seven unethical practices in this study:

- There was no informed consent
- The participants were not informed of all the known dangers.
- The participants had to agree to an autopsy after their death, in order to have their funeral costs covered.
- Scientists denied treatment to some patients, in order to observe the individual dangers and fatal progression of the disease.

- Participants were not given the cure, even when it was widely known and easily available.
- The designers used a misleading advertisement: The researchers advertised for participants with the slogan; *Last Chance for Special Free Treatment.* The subjects were, however, not given a treatment, instead they were recruited for a very risky spinal tap-diagnostic.
- The scientists did not follow the commonly used ethical rules of research.

The Belmont Report

As a result of the abuses brought to light from the Tuskegee Syphilis Study, the *U.S. Public Health Service* created the *Belmont Report* (Office of the Secretary, 1979), for the protection of human subject testing:

- <u>Respect for persons</u>—protecting the autonomy of all people and treating them with courtesy and respect and allowing for informed consent. Researchers must be truthful and conduct no deception;
- <u>Beneficence</u>—The philosophy of *do no harm* while maximizing benefits for the research project and minimizing risks to the research subjects; and
- <u>Justice</u>—ensuring reasonable, non-exploitative, and well-considered procedures are administered fairly; the fair distribution of costs and benefits to *potential* research participants and equally.

Today, to ensure compliance with the *Belmont Report*, medical facilities and university settings which conduct research involving human subjects are required to have an *Institutional Review Board* (IRB). The purpose of the IRB is to not only assure that ethical and legal steps are taken to protect the rights e.g., informed consent, but also to protect participants from any physical or psychological harm they might be exposed to in the research. Still, there may be some ambiguity regarding *how* such measures are to be interpreted, let alone carried out. Therefore, in order to ensure the rights of participants in a bio-medical clinical study, there are practical steps caregivers can provide such as ensure that the patient understands the full extent of the experiment and informed consent, support a person's privacy of his/her identity, their motivation to participate or refusal being in the experiment, etc. (Sims, 2010). Yet despite improvements in the fair treatment and ethical procedures in human subject testing, many feared that the Tuskegee Study may have irreversibly damaged public trust for medical research. For example, one such study from John Hopkins University in 2002, focused on African Americans' negative perceptions of being included in any future trials. Such perceptions included their reluctance of being abused, not being asked to be participants in future studies compared to other ethnic people, and their chances of being harmed. Johns Hopkins internist and epidemiologist, Neil R. Powe, M.D., echoes this sentiment as he understands that the tragedy of Tuskegee now lies in the likelihood that *African Americans will be left out of important findings about the latest treatments for diseases, especially those that take a greater toll on African Americans and consequently may not have ready or equal access to the latest medicines.*

Truth and Reconciliation Commissions

> *Truth and reconciliation commissions, perhaps more than any other function, serve to answer the many unanswered questions generated by enforced disappearances, extrajudicial executions and other crimes committed in times of State unresponsiveness and*

*secrecy, that leave relatives wondering what happened to
the victims and where they might be.*

International Justice Resource Center, 2016

After apartheid was abolished in South Africa, a Truth and
Reconciliation Commission (TRC) was established by President
Nelson Mandela in 1994. Chaired by Archbishop Desmond Tutu,
victims and survivors gave their testimonies about human rights
violations they suffered under apartheid between 1960 and 1994.
Perpetrators of such crimes under apartheid rule were also allowed
to testify about their abusive activities, and request amnesty from
any civil and criminal prosecution if they could prove that they were
following orders at the time. South Africa's TRC was the first truth
commission to offer amnesty to individuals who fully disclosed in
public their involvement in politically motivated crimes (Chapman
and van der Merwe, 2008). Some of the testimonies of the victims
and survivors included:

- Killing parents in front of children. Killing children in front
  of parents.
- Raping women and children.
- Cutting off the hands of victims so they were unable to be
  fingerprinted and identified later.
- Pulling out moustaches, beards, teeth and tongues.
- Administered electric shocks to genital areas.
- Destruction of property, forced relocations and detainment.

Although these stories were very painful to hear and recount,
the purpose of the TRC of South Africa was two-fold: One, it was
designed to follow a model of *restorative justice* (focusing on the
needs of the victims, offenders, and the community) style instead
of the *retributive justice* (the response to a crime is proportionate to
the punishment) style that characterized the Nuremberg trials. Two,
the goal of the TRC was to prevent such atrocities from reoccurring

while at the same time, unify a deeply divided nation scarred by apartheid. However, 10 years after the TRC report was issued a group of South African and American researchers, Stein, Seedat, Moomal and Herman (2008) reviewed the impact of the TRC on psychological distress and found that South Africans generally viewed the TRC as only *moderately positive*. Why might this be? Perhaps the answers lie in the fact that the well-intended process of reconciliation could only do so much. Perhaps it simply was not enough for victims/survivors to be heard. Perhaps there were not enough socio-economic-financial resources to carry out the TRC's recommendations to effect change in the socio-political system.

These days, it often appears to be in vogue to jump on the band wagons of Truth and Reconciliation Commissions as they seek to make amends for human rights violations.

> *In the aftermath of massive human rights abuses, victims have well established rights to see the perpetrators punished, to know the truth, and to receive reparations. Because systemic human rights violations affect not just the direct victims, but society as a whole, in addition to satisfying these obligations, states have duties to guarantee that the violations will not recur, and therefore, a special duty to reform institutions that were either involved in or incapable of preventing the abuses.*
>
> The International Center for Transitional Justice, (2017)

TRC's often hold public hearings in which victims/survivors can share their stories, and sometimes, confront their former abusers. The goal of these hearings sometimes includes the hope of forgiveness for past crimes, and the hope that society can heal, and be made whole again (Bakiner, 2016). Amstutz (2005) notes how, on one hand, TRC's are committed to uncover historical accounts that promote truth, but also their work may unknowingly contribute to further wounding victims and survivors. For example,

- TRC's have difficulties in defining forgiveness and reconciliation on a community level, and often concentrate instead on relationships between individual victims and perpetrators.
- Testimonies from victims and family members are often pressured to share their stories of abuse, and those who did were not persuaded to forgive perpetrators.
- Perpetrators were reluctant to acknowledge their actions, offer meaningful apologies, express regret, and/or offer some form of compensation to those who had suffered.

However, Hamber (1996) cautions that a TRC needs to be structured on a *survivor-centered approach*, otherwise public hearings and events can, ironically, obstruct the healing of individuals and communities. In fact, there is an inherent risk involved for victims and survivors telling their stories, because not only do these testimonies become the basis for a TRC's final report, but also public reconciliation processes often promote impunity for crimes committed (Amstutz, 2005). For example, when the *Truth and Reconciliation Commission of Canada* held its National Event in Vancouver in 2013, many criticized this public gathering as deliberately down-playing the frequency and severity of the physical, emotional, psychological and spiritual atrocities committed in these schools by the Roman Catholic, Anglican Church of Canada, United Church of Canada, Presbyterian, Congregationalist, and Methodist churches (Miller, 1996). Attendees also noticed that there were no exhibits related to the documented evidence (Moore, 1942) regarding the exposure of the deplorable living conditions of these schools, diseases deliberately brought upon the children, pictures of dead bodies and uncovered mass graves. In all actuality, such testimonies and documentations were included in the final report of the TRC. Nevertheless, such an event intended to promote truth and healing which misrepresents facts, ultimately misleads the public who may be unfamiliar with the 120-year history of Canadian aboriginal residential schools. Furthermore, critics alleged that such a public event violated International Law regarding the involvement of governments and institutions that are complicit in crimes against humanity, are not permitted to dictate any terms of recovery, justice or legal resolutions (Lemmens, 2013).

Minow's (1998) work *Between Vengeance and Forgiveness: Facing History after Genocide and Mass Violence,* has defined measurable objectives for what a TRC's role should achieve, such as creating public awareness of atrocities, obtain full accounts to build a record for history, transform violence into the practice of respect that restores dignity to victims and survivors, punish offenders for their crimes, build an international order to try to prevent, and also, to respond to aggression, torture, and atrocities, etc. Sherman and Strang (2007) note that there are several positive outcomes to seeking *restorative justice,* such as it helps reduce recidivism and post-traumatic stress symptoms, as well as increases satisfaction that justice had been served. Moreover, unlike *retributive justice* that determines if the response to a crime is proportionate to the punishment, *restorative justice* focuses on repairing the harm caused by criminal behavior. In an ideal situation, a mediator helps facilitate a cooperative effort from both sides address the wrongdoing and the harm caused to others. However, this collaboration does not imply that the offender of such crimes dictates the terms of reconciliation. Instead, the impact of the crimes committed are seen for the harm they caused others, as well as work toward attainable solutions that will bring about lasting reconciliation. In this way, transformational healing is given an opportunity to take root in all people, relationships and communities; past, present and future.

CHAPTER SIX

Vaya con Dios

Where It All Began: Montauk, Long Island: NY

As I started to become more aware of soul consciousness at an early age, I began to hear the cries of the wounded in very distinct ways, e.g., muffled cries and sobs in various states of consciousness. This awareness, I believe, was not by accident. In fact, my Native American Indian teacher, who pointed out my cut finger in his *blood and ancestors lesson*, awakened me further on this journey to release the souls that had been trapped by trauma. To accomplish this, it was no longer sufficient for me to simply hear their cries, but it was time for me to visit the physical places that witnessed these crimes against humanity. It was now time to transform traumatic energies, heal the land, and release these souls back to God.

Early on in my counselor training I had learned that when a loved-one dies, part of the process of grief work involved disconnecting our emotional energy from a deceased loved-one and reconnecting our emotional energy to other *living* relationships. Sigmund Freud in his famous work *Mourning and Melancholia* (1917) proposed a concept of grief work that required a person to perform a very distinct mental task, i.e., a *cathexis*, or a release of one's mental energy holding an object or person. For example, when the *object* of our love ceased to exist (e.g., mother, father, etc.), the person became conscious of the loss, and the emotional attachment (libido) would then be required to withdraw that energy from the deceased person/object. I like to think of Freud's concept as a burned-out light-socket. Let's say that you plug a lamp into a light socket that does not work. The lamp is fine, but you discover that there is no electricity being supplied to run your lights or other appliances. Therefore, it only makes sense to find another outlet that supplies electrical current. An example of this *cathexis* might be when a widow/widower starts to date or marries again. She/he may still have feelings for the deceased spouse but has reconnected their emotional and physical energies into new relationships. All in all, Freud's work helped researchers begin to understand that mourning was and is a process; an emotional, psychological, physical and spiritual working through the loss of a loved-one. Since then, there has been numerous paradigms that explain the process of grief and mourning, e.g., Eric Lindemann (1979), Elizabeth Kubler Ross (2014), William Worden (2018), etc.

Several years before I had that life-changing cut on my finger, my Native American Indian teacher was already preparing me for this new way of transmuting negative traumatic energy. I was invited to assist him and two others to perform a healing ceremony at Camp Hero State Park in Montauk, Long Island, New York. Again, I had not yet experienced releasing any souls trapped by tragedy, let alone intergenerational trauma. Besides its beautiful coastline, Montauk had often been linked to many suspect activities involving the development of time travel and mind-control experiments throughout World War II (Nichols and Moon, 1992). Although never proven, eyewitnesses reported that the United States government developed a powerfully new psychological weapon that could drive their enemies insane, by producing schizophrenic-like symptoms at the push of a button. Accordingly, people who were considered *expendable,* were abducted and transported to the base where they underwent excruciating periods of both physical and mental torture (Bielek, 2000). On a sunny Saturday afternoon in January, the small group of us walked the State Park grounds for a couple of hours, until my teacher pointed to an open field approximately 100 yards from the AN/FPS-35 radar dish. There, we would conduct our healing ceremony. As we marked off the grid and prepared ourselves with prayers, we could feel the negative spiritual energy beneath our feet. My chest felt heavy as the weight of years of oppression in the victims were palpable. We marked off a circle, and I followed my teacher's lead. When he started to offer prayers in his native tongue, suddenly his knees buckled, and I remember catching him from collapsing to the ground. In that moment, we all felt a *swoosh* of energy blowing upwards, I was told later that what we actually felt was the land releasing its trauma and souls that were bound there. This energy released seemed to go on for hours. When the process was over, we finished our ceremony by blessing the land with more prayers, tobacco and sage offerings. Later that day, tears flowed from my teacher's eyes as he told us that he felt all the anguish and pain these experiments caused the people, including the enormous negative energy the land released when the trapped souls went to be with God. He described the people in great detail and the psychological experiments conducted on them. To this day, he still gets choked up when he recalls this experience.

Prayers at Bear Butte and Wounded Knee

Since that initial lesson with my Native American teacher, my soul has been called to various places to offer prayers for trapped souls to be healed and released. At times, I have been privileged to witness the souls being released by the land and return to God, and other times, I have initiated the prayers so that others may complete the release later. Either way, I have learned that this work has no room for ego, but rather a humility that calls for one to listen carefully to the ancestors' voices, as well as stirring of the Soul of the Universe. For example, months before my fifth pilgrimage to Bear Butte, I started to have dreams about the souls of Native American Indian children standing around the base of this sacred site. There were various tribes, e.g., Lakota, Cheyenne, Dakota, Crow, Hunkpapa, etc. Unlike my previous trips that were for my own spiritual awareness and renewal (read *Reclaiming Authenticity,* Houck, 2014), this time these children were waiting for me to come and climb the mountain with them. I sensed that I was going to be part helping them go with God, however none of them appeared to be wounded by trauma. Perhaps they were the generations trapped by all of the horrific energy from the bloodshed and misery brought upon their people from the United States government. Regardless, the closer the time came for me to leave for South Dakota, the more the children started to sing and play in my dreams. In fact, when I reached Bear Butte, their voices were quite deafening. I can still hear their laughter and songs in my soul to this day. Standing at the bottom of Bear Butte, I offered many prayers and made tobacco/sage ties for gratitude and healing. As I started to climb, I saw the children climbing with me; some running on ahead, others following behind. Along the way, I would occasionally stop, catch my breath, and hang prayer ties on the branches of trees. As we reached the top, the souls of these children, one by one, were whisked away to heaven, as if entering a powerful vortex. Again, I offered more prayer ties of tobacco and sage for all Native American Indians as a means of asking forgiveness for past atrocities, offering gratitude for their friendship and sowing the seeds of peace and love. When I returned to my motel room later that day in Sturgis, I remember being physically exhausted and I slept for the rest of the day. The next morning, I returned to the southern base of Bear Butte. There were people already climbing the mountain, so I offered more prayers and drummed softly as I watched others reach the top. Interestingly, I could faintly hear their joyful songs from those at the top, waving their staffs, eagle and hawk feathers, and colorful tobacco offerings. I smiled as I sensed the joy of these fellow climbers, not so much from reaching the top, but that they were aware of being part of something bigger, namely the healing of generations. Even the land felt lighter that morning.

The following day I traveled south to the Wounded Knee Cemetery, where approximately 300 Native America Indians had been killed and buried in a mass grave. According to history, following the arrest and killing of Chief Sitting Bull, the 7th Calvary set out to capture Big Foot's people fleeing to Pine Ridge (Coleman, 2000).

This pursuit was to finally put an end to the Ghost Dance Movement, and other *perceived* accounts of insurrection against the United States. When the Calvary caught up to Big Foot's camp on December 29, 1890, they attempted to confiscate weapons from the people. All of sudden, a single shot rang out, and within seconds, the Calvary began to fire volley after volley into the Sioux, Miniconjou and Hunkpapa camp. Native American Indian men rushed to retrieve their confiscated rifles, while the women and children ran for a ravine near the camp, only to be cut down in crossfire. Some historians believe the reason the 7th Calvary attacked Big Foot's people was to take revenge for their regiment's defeat at Little Bighorn in 1876 (Hall, 1991). Nevertheless, following the killing of Sitting Bull and the attack at Wounded Knee, the United States Army awarded 20 medals of honor to its soldiers (Andersson, 2009). As a result, Wounded Knee was hailed as the last major confrontation in the United States' war against the Sioux. To this day, the Cemetery serves as a painful reminder of a government's action of 1890. I replayed this account in my mind as I sat on a hillside just a stone's throw from this gravesite. I stuck feathers in the ground with tobacco and sage to honor the souls there. That day my prayers were very simple: *I asked for the release of the souls still trapped by the tragedy, not exclusively within the Cemetery itself, but also for the pain and oppression that is still evident throughout the surrounding communities and extended reservations.*

The Mohawk Institute

I have never met anyone who has ever fully tasted the love, mercy and grace of God and not be changed by it. In fact, when people have a direct experience of God through prayer, meditation or miracle, eventually this *vertical* relationship shows up in *horizontal*, interpersonal relationships. For example, the more people experience the grace of God in their lives, the kinder and more compassionate they become toward the vulnerable and weak in society. This is not to

James A. Houck, Jr., Ph.D.

say that people who have a direct encounter with God have the right, or *street credit*, to boast about it. Quite the contrary. When anyone has such an experience with God that turns their world spiritually upside down and inside out, they often become very humbled as a result. In other words, their compassion grows towards themselves, and their gratitude, mercy and love evidently extend to others.

Yet, the more we come to understand the patterns and history of crimes against humanity, the collusion between church and state-run agencies to commit and cover up atrocities, and the trauma that continues to be passed down through the generations, the more it becomes obvious that both victims *and* perpetrators need to be healed and released from their trauma. Just as people who suffer from intergenerational trauma struggle to break free from their persecution, oppression and victimization, so too do perpetrators suffer from intergenerational patterns of entitlement, narcissism, coercion, intimidation and violence. While it is true that everyone is held accountable for their thoughts, words and deeds, nonetheless, one's emotional, psychological and spiritual pain is there just below the surface. In other words, considering the depths people go to inflict harm on others, their own trauma and pain is always lower. The reason for this phenomenon is that attitudes of contempt, anger and violence toward others, serve to protect a person's wounds from being touched. In other words, the greater the violence, the deeper the emotional, psychological and spiritual pain. Therefore, perhaps perpetrators acted in cruel and inhumane ways, because they themselves were unconsciously, or consciously, acting out of their own traumatic pasts?

Interestingly, this was the lesson I learned when I felt called to pray for souls of children, whose remains were discovered on the grounds of the Mohawk Institute in Brantford, Ontario. Weeks prior to this visit, I researched the history of the Institute and discovered various stories of children whose deaths were never accounted for by the Church. In fact, outsiders had unearthed sections of the grounds believed to be part of mass graves (Annett, 2011). They found articles of children's clothing, porcelain buttons of school uniforms, ribbons and even pieces of children's bones. These physical evidences only reinforced the stories from adult survivors of the Mohawk Institute about the mistreatment, exploitation and physical, emotional and sexual abuse children suffered.

Prior to my trip to Brantford, my dreams consisted of hearing the souls of these children laughing and crying. Upon arriving at the Mohawk Institute, their songs became stronger as my soul trembled with anticipation. I sat on the grounds behind the abandoned main building for some time to feel the energy. The air was a mixture of sorrowfulness and relief. I had made prayer ties of tobacco and sage that were hung at the edge of the woods about 50 yards from the school. Taking my drum, I began to walk around the grounds softly drumming and asked for God's assistance for the universe to surround me with love and grace. I asked to speak to the souls of the children who remained tied to the land, that it was time for them to go be with God. Their sorrow and sobs quickly turned into sounds of laughter, just like I heard in my dreams weeks before. I continued to walk the grounds and drum, telling these souls that they were not forgotten, and God knows every one of them by name. I told them that God has heard their cries, and the trauma that they suffered at this place is now being healed; they no longer are tied to this land because the negative energy of trauma has been broken. I started to see the children's souls come up out of the woods, dressed in their school uniforms. The girls had ribbons in their hair and the boys were wearing white shirts. Sometimes they would come up individually, or sometimes two by two. Once they reached the edge of the woods, they looked up and were immediately transported to heaven. After some time, I was also led to pray for the healing and release of the souls who committed such atrocities. I prayed not only for their release from the land, but for the perpetrators to be healed from their own intergenerational trauma that influenced them to mistreat and kill indigenous children. I felt a shift of energy in the land, almost as if it gave a huge sigh of relief. The air was definitely lighter and more peaceful now.

James A. Houck, Jr., Ph.D.

The Mass Graves in Ireland

From the experience at the Mohawk Institute, I became aware of other crimes against humanity throughout the world in which there was a secret collusion between the government and the church. I stumbled across the story of Tuam, County Galway, Ireland where there had been a discovery of approximately 800 remains of babies buried in a mass grave. There were also stories of child abuse and burials that emerged from the mother-child home in Bessboro, County Cork. I contacted the people in Ireland working to bring about awareness and accountability of these places to the government and church. I shared with them how their stories of the mistreatment of women, the abuse of children, and the mass burials, paralleled Native American Indians' experiences with United States and Canadian boarding schools. We were both astonished to find that in spite of the striking parallels, neither of us knew about each other country's atrocities. To our amazement, it was almost as if these global crimes against humanity formed a recurring pattern of humanity that was being played out in other places.

When I visited Cork, I interviewed several women who were born and raised at the Bessboro Mother-Child Home. I heard women's stories of punishment and abuses which appeared to be a daily occurrence in the state-religious run institution. There had also been reports of collaboration of the townsfolks, who would often return young runaway mothers back to the Home. Apparently, there was an underlying belief that those girls who became pregnant out of wedlock, were sent to these facilities to work off their *sins*. As reported by some of the women I interviewed, surrounding communities also sent support perhaps in order to rid society and church of wayward girls. As a result, children born to these mothers, were viewed as illegitimate and therefore not allowed to be baptized by the church. Furthermore, young mothers were further alienated from their communities, as they were forbidden to be *churched*, a term meaning the blessing given to new mothers after recovery from childbirth in order to receive the sacraments again (Knodel, 1995). In addition, since children born out of wedlock were illegitimate, they could easily be assimilated into the adoption/foster care system, without their mother's consent, which also provided a nice income for the church.

Bessboro Mother-Child Home

Courtyard at Bessboro Mother-Child Home
County Cork, Ireland

As I walked these grounds, I sensed an oppressive burden that hung over these souls like a huge spider's web. In nature, spiders are able to spin both sticky and non-sticky silk threads. By doing so, spiders avoid getting caught in their own web, all the while their prey are trapped. Ironically, this image is an accurate description of the way individuals feel trapped by a government/religious system; once caught in this web of assumptions, prejudices and penalties, the more victims struggled, the more they became entangled. With this image in mind, I passed a little memorial garden that was behind the Mother-Child Home. There were stones that marked some of the babies buried there, as well as some markers for some nuns who were also buried there. To the sides of this garden appeared to be other places where the ground had been disturbed. It was reported that the unmarked graves of children were there. After I hung my traditional tobacco and sage prayer ties in the trees, I sat down and began to play my Native American Indian flute. This time, I allowed the sound of the flute to pray for the healing and release of the children and their mothers, whose souls were trapped in this spider's web. I also prayed for the release of the adult community who still suffer the effects of being adopted and are unable to connect with their real families. Interestingly, this is the first time that I started to see the strong connection between not only those who were victims and the pain that they carried in their intergenerational trauma, but I also saw this trauma in the people who ran such institutions. Therefore, I also prayed for those who out of their own trauma, were guilty of inflicting such pain, suffering and contempt on others. Perhaps the church and state officials had been struggling with their own intergenerational trauma and were unable to offer the depth of God's love they never experienced. Perhaps instead of dealing compassionately with young girls who were *in trouble,* these religious orders justified their methods as punishment for the sins of infidelity. Perhaps those who ran such institutions had been raised to believe that God was/is a punishing God, and that their own lives mirrored this oppressive, strict and fearful relationship. If one was not careful to remain *pure,* God would strike you dead. Therefore, perhaps they *wounded* others out of their *wounds* that had been passed down through generations that was reinforced by a system that encouraged control over them and the lives of others.

Crough Patrick, County Mayo, Ireland

I decided to end my trip in Ireland by climbing Crough Patrick, considered one of the holiest mountains in Ireland. It is said that in 441 AD, St. Patrick fasted 40 days on this mountain

As I climbed the rocky path, I hung more prayer ties on the trees and shrubs, offering gratitude for God not only hearing the cries of all souls, but also for the healing of those who have been waiting to be fully reconnected. Early that morning it had rained, and so I was unable to reach the top. The moisture made the shale rocks very slippery. Yet, as I was coming down from the mountain, I met an elderly couple on their way up who looked like experienced climbers. We chatted for a moment, when all of a sudden, the gentleman said, *Wow, would you look at that!* and pointed for me to look over my shoulder. I turned around and saw the most beautiful rainbow coming off the mountain and going down into the bay. In a moment, I felt an overwhelming sense of bliss and peace wash over me. It was as if God reminded me that generations will no longer suffer in silence, because oppressive spider's webs are being dismantled and transformed into beautiful rainbows.

Rainbow at Crough Patrick
Mountain County Mayo, Ireland

CHAPTER SEVEN

Liberating Ancestors,
Liberating Ourselves

We shall not cease from exploration.
And the end of all our exploring will be to arrive where
we started and know the place for the first time.

T. S. Elliot, *Little Gidding*

As a counseling educator, clinician and pastoral professional, I am often saddened by people's beliefs that when it comes to addressing their physical, emotional and spiritual problems, they consider themselves powerless and without a voice. Perhaps this is a result of never feeling valued or never allowed to use their voice. Admittedly, many people are unable to perceive their insights and strengths, as if they cannot see themselves capable of healing, let alone, achieving anything meaningful with their lives. Most of the time, people are content to live for brief moments of joy and celebration, marked off by transitional milestones of baptisms, marriages, birthdays, graduations, promotions, retirements, etc. Furthermore, when it comes to wrestling with life's questions, many people are often overwhelmed not only by the concept that the answers they seek often lie within themselves, but also the belief that inner freedom, peace, joy and unconditional love, are all too good to be true. For example, one of the major *psycho-social-spiritual* obstacles I run into when counseling others occurs when emotionally wounded people are genuinely frightened and immobilized by their potential for healing and inner growth. As we explore their painful memories, people often catch a glimpse of what healing and wholeness might look like for them. When this insight occurs, they may be tempted to sabotage themselves by falling back into old ways in order to avoid embracing what healing requires of them, e.g., forgiveness, letting go of bitterness, resentment, etc. Even when an opportunity to forgive and reconcile with one who has caused great pain and suffering (and vice versa) is presented, because bitterness has so entangled their souls, it is often impossible to let go of their pain. In other words, sometimes both the victim/survivor and offenders cannot envision taking hold of something better; it is just too vulnerable of a place for them to go.

Indeed, forgiving, freeing, reclaiming and embracing the potential of one's life does require courage, openness, and a shift in thinking from a linear process, to a more open-ended, expansive perception of time and space. Although each person walks his/her own path, embracing forgiveness, healing, grace, and love occurs as each person is ready. No one can do this for another; the door of healing can be shown, but one must turn the key and walk through. Most of the time, there is a strong connection between this perception of fear and powerlessness and a lifetime of low to no self-esteem. Through various hurtful experiences, people have internalized society's definition that they are *dirty, worthless, dispensable, no-good, backward, will amount to nothing,* etc. Although it is difficult to say *when* people started to internalize such messages, it is perhaps easier to pinpoint *from whom* these messages came. History certainly has demonstrated that society holds out an ever-changing measuring stick that has one standard for the so-called privileged, and another for the weakened and wounded. Nevertheless, regardless of its place in history, there seems to be a continuous pattern of interpersonal indignity and humiliation for people who do not realize their truth and have been convinced that the only way to know themselves, is to settle on society's definition and mistreatment of them. Unfortunately, for some wounded people, that is enough to settle for.

Admittedly, looking to others for approval and self-worth appears to be a natural part of developing a sense of who we are. In fact, this behavior is often how we first learn about ourselves, others and the world. Families, teachers, and other early childhood authority figures reflect their own views and mirror these perceptions back to us. For example, long before we could form words, we are skilled at reading facial prompts, sensing another's approval or disapproval, recognizing tones of love, laughter, anger and contempt, distinguishing between a loving touch or a cold detachment, and learning every other emotion in between. Moreover, sometime around three months of age, we began to engage in face-to-face interactions with our caregivers; a social referencing as it were. As infants, we display visual, facial, and vocal behaviors in response to how we are being treated, through a kind of *give-and-take* exchange between ourselves and others, typically to help us understand different situations (Feldman, 2007). Thus, we hold these initial interactions in our bodies, as we developed a sense of trust and safety, or suspicion and distrust. From these early stages of infancy, we learned to regulate our affect as we took our social cues from the people around us, i.e., *how* to express our feelings appropriately, as well as *when* and *where* such emotions are to be displayed (e.g., at work, play, school, family celebrations, funerals, etc.). As we physically and emotionally mature, we must learn to become less dependent on others for this directional affirmation, and replace it with an internalized, or individual, sense of who we are. In other words, instead of looking externally to get what we need in terms of approval and acceptance, we now look within to find such qualities, i.e., resiliency, peace, self-love, etc.

Nevertheless, let us keep in mind that just as we initially looked to others for our sense of affirmation, belonging and acceptance, so too are others looking to us to *receive* their sense of affirmation, belonging and acceptance. At first glance, this exchange appears to be mutually beneficial, however, it can also lead to co-dependency in all our relationships. For example, co-dependency is typically seen in an unhealthy relationship whereby one person supports or enables another person's addiction, poor mental health, immaturity, irresponsibility, insecurity or under-achievement, to name a few. Perhaps the most common theme in co-dependency is this excessive reliance on others for one's approval and sense of identity (Johnson,

2014). Understandably, people simply do not know who they are apart from their dependence on another's emotional need to physically, psychologically, emotionally, and spiritually define, and thus, control them. Since most people tend to have an underdeveloped sense of who they are, they not only have yet to believe in a healthier, stronger potential that lies within, but also, they mirror an incomplete reflection of themselves, and vice versa. Such perceptions are simply distorted mirroring of our underdeveloped, limited life experiences of how we view God, the world, others and ourselves.

In Hans Christian Andersen's children story, *The Snow Princess* (1845), an evil troll, a.k.a. the devil, uses a very large magic mirror (like fun house mirrors at carnivals) to distort the appearance of everything it reflects. In fact, the mirror was not designed to reflect the wholesome and beautiful aspects of people and things, but instead, magnifies only their ugly and wicked characteristics. Throughout the story, the troll becomes amused in distorting the images of everyone and everything, to the degree that even the most beautiful lands reflect *boiled spinach*. One day, the troll decides, with the help of his minions, to carry the mirror into heaven so that he might make fools of the angels and God. However, the mirror slips from their grasp and falls back to earth, shattering into billions of pieces. These miniscule shards are then blown by the wind all over the Earth which get into people's eyes and hearts. As a result, people's hearts become frozen like ice, and their eyes can now only see the ugliness and evil in each other and the world in which they live.

Ironically, intergenerational trauma presents striking parallels regarding Andersen's story in that what has been handed down to us through our ancestors, are often the shards of distorted perceptions of who we truly are as souls, as well as what *freezes* our hearts from seeing the beauty and goodness in all people. For our ancestors who have suffered crimes against humanity, society has often held up its own mirrors of misleading standards; sometimes intentionally and sometimes unintentionally. Nevertheless, the *shards of illusion* are intentionally designed to add generational distortions to the eyes and hearts of the wounded. Over time then, our minds tell us that what we perceive, albeit limited and hazy, must be true. Groebecker (2008) echoes this sentiment as she states that people are born with certain tendencies of the mind that condition us to be ignorant of our true selves. In fact, as trauma is passed down genetically, it attaches itself to our DNA and often covertly disguises itself as harmful physical, psychological, emotional and spiritual symptoms. Similarly, as intergenerational trauma is passed down through society and families, i.e., *what we carry in our genes, how we are/were raised, etc.,* various social systems also galvanize harmful stereotypes, prejudices, injustices, emotional dependence, biases, etc. Therefore, intergenerational trauma is not just limited to how it affects our families, but also affects all relationships, from the most intimate to the mere acquaintances in our lives.

Still, when there have been crimes against humanity resulting in mass graves from genocide, government and religious cover ups and scandals, social injustices, oppression, torture, etc., suggests a uniqueness to intergenerational trauma that stains both the souls of the living and the deceased. For example, the deceased often become stuck in their trauma, unable to move on from where their death occurred. This is because the land has been imprinted with the horrors of genocide and desolation, to the extent that the blood of those who have laid slain cry out from the land (Genesis 4:10). We may attempt to forget about these tragedies, as the so-called history books are written from a softer perspective that romanticizes the harsh reminders of the depraved human interaction (Houck, 2014). However, antiquity echoes beyond the grave voices of pain and suffering that compel us that their stories need to be heard and told.

Bread Crumbs

The window for healing intergenerational trauma is never limited by time and space because the soul is not bound by such things.

Seeing intergenerational trauma for what it is then, not only releases our ancestors, ourselves and future generations from its agonizing grip of finality, but also empowers us to fully embrace ourselves as soul. Therefore, when it comes to listening to the painful cries of our ancestors, the only questions we need to ask ourselves are: *Do we truly trust that we are the generation who can transform trauma in our ancestors when we are healed, and can we be transformed through their healing?* Our ancestors certainly think so. After all, consider…

- Why are we the ones who know about the atrocities done to them?
- Why are we the ones who hear their cries to be released from their pain and trauma?
- Why are we the ones who hear their cries to be connected and/or reconnected with God?
- Why me? Why do I have to be the one who deals with all of this pain?
- Why couldn't I have been born into another family?
- Why couldn't they stop this pain from being passed down through the family?
- Why did this abusive/addictive cycle have to continue?

The answer to these questions is simple: *Our ancestors may not have been psychologically, physically, emotionally and/or spiritually strong enough to heal and transform their trauma. We are.* Our ancestors look to us now because we are the ones who can transform family trauma. This ancestral request is worth serious consideration. In fact, perhaps our ancestors get our attention through some of our physical, emotional, psychological and spiritual struggles that were similar to theirs. Perhaps our present manifestations of intergenerational trauma also indicate how, when, where, and why our ancestors were unable to heal in their lives? Nonetheless, I believe that they are now asking for our help.

Regardless of how we try to make sense of the intergenerational trauma phenomena, our ancestors do speak to us. In fact, the more we come into our own soul consciousness, the more fully we can embrace our truth that we have everything we need to transform negative and harmful energies of dysfunctional systems by our actions of truth, understanding, compassion, forgiveness, gratitude and love. These traits are no longer to be treated as mere buzz words spoken in educational, political and/or religious venues, but rather, once we develop, integrate and anchor these characteristics in our lives, they become powerful forces that transmute others from their hidden, voiceless pain and suffering, into liberated souls no longer bound by traumatic experiences. Ours' is an *experiential* relationship with God, and therefore, urges us to embrace others as they have experienced life. Therefore, in seeking to heal from our own intergenerational wounds, I believe we must first recognize and remove the distorted shards of prejudices and misperceptions from society's mirror, in order to do so for the rest of humanity. Indeed, a major teaching of Jesus occurred one day when he asked his followers:

> *Why do you look at the speck of sawdust in your brother's*
> *eye and pay no attention to the plank in your own eye?*
> *How can you say to your brother, 'Let me take the speck*
> *out of your eye', when all the time there is a plank in your*
> *own eye…first take the plank out of your own eye, and*
> *then you will see clearly to remove the speck from your*
> *brother's eye.* Matthew 7:3-5

Healing intergenerational trauma calls for us to deal with both ourselves and others in a compassionate manner. For example, as we trace our ancestral wounds back to generations who suffered horrors and injustices, it is not a matter of placing blame at the feet of our ancestors, distant or recent, for what they passed down to us. True, each soul is accountable for their lifetime on earth. However, the purpose in listening to our ancestors is to first and foremost acknowledge the blood and soul connection we have with them.

When we are able to do so, we not only honor their lives, but also sow the seeds of compassion, understanding and peace in all.

In the Tiwa Pueblo Indian tradition there is a ceremony called the Drum Dance. Each year these *Dances* are held throughout the world and are the result of the teachings of Joseph Rale, Beautiful Painted Arrow. In his book, *Being and Vibration* (2015), Joseph explains the origins and purpose of this Dance:

> *I was given a vision in which I saw a Drum Dance. Men and women dancers were moving rhythmically back and forth on an open field from inside a giant drum that was being played ... The drum was made from a hollow log with a skin on it. The people who were playing the drum said that when doing a Drum Dance, the dancers would bring forth greatness because the wood is greatness and is what the drum is made from. The dancers would dance the vibration of the sound, bouncing back (present) and forth (future) and returning to past memory, like the sound waves which were bouncing back and forth inside the hollow log of the drum being played. This would be a way by which all physical life would pick up the resonating vibration of sound by which to shift consciousness. This could create the necessary planetary changes because the planetary energies wanted to dance effortlessly between the present, future, and memory of harmony ...*
>
> *During the first day, the dancers release emotional hindrances to their personal growth ... By the second day, fatigue starts to set in. As the physical body surrenders, there is . . . a sense of exhilaration, of transcending limitations and beliefs about oneself. The dancers begin to receive glimpses of other parallel realities. During the third day, a golden plate forms over the heads of the*

*dancers and another plate appears directly below on the
ground at the feet of the dancers. From time to time, the
energy spirals from the lower plate to the upper plate,
connecting the Earth energy with the Sky energy...*

I myself have danced several of these dances, with each one creating a new and wonderful experience for me. Yet, there was one particular year when I became acutely aware of the blood and soul connection I had with my ancestors both in the past, as well as those yet to be born. For example, it was on the second day when I had been dancing forwards and backwards for some time. All of a sudden, I no longer felt as though I was performing the movements. Every time I danced forward, it seemed as though I was being pushed in that direction by all the future generations; children, grandchildren, great grandchildren, etc., yet to be born. When I danced backwards, it seemed as though I was being pulled in that direction by those who have come before me. All in all, I was experiencing an ancestral healing that exceeded time and space. As time went on, the more I danced, the more I rested in this blood and soul connection that carried me along.

Like me with my Native American Indian teacher, most people have not given much thought to their ancestors as they look at their blood. Despite the fact that our ancestors lived in different times and places, they are not so unlike us. After all, we do share the same DNA, and by knowing our own physical, psychological, emotional, and spiritual struggles, we may come to better understand theirs. Moreover, perhaps just like us...

- Our ancestors may have been overwhelmed to the point that their resiliency was quickly exhausted, or perhaps it was chipped away over time by relentless oppression.
- Our ancestors had to do what they had to do (not being necessarily proud of what they did) to survive, defend and raise families, make ends meet, etc.

- Our ancestors did not always make the best decisions, or even consider the impact their decisions had on their relationships, especially those who have yet to be born.
- Our ancestors never considered additional physical, psychological, emotional or spiritual burdens that were placed on others because of how they benefitted or were burdened.
- Our ancestors may have abused drugs or alcohol, or struggled with other addictions, because it was the only perceived available thing they had to hold themselves together, which only made matters worse for themselves and their families.
- Our ancestors were unaware of the psychological and emotional roles they played in order to unconsciously maintain the daily chaos, co-dependency, confusion and self-sabotage behaviors typically found in families with addictions?
- Our ancestors attempted or completed suicide because their emotional pain and hopelessness was too great for them to see any other way through their problems.
- Our ancestors initiated a cycle of physical, emotional or sexual abuse out of their own experiences of being ridiculed, abused, beaten, and shamed. On the other hand, some of our ancestors may have been the abusers, striking fear in the hearts of others through extortion, greed, manipulation, violence and oppression.
- Our ancestors were guilty of pulling triggers or exploding bombs that ended the lives of many.
- Our ancestors may have turned a blind eye to society's wounded and so-called insignificant people that were being oppressed, shunned, tortured, and killed, as their hands held the shovels that opened and closed the earth for mass graves.
- Our ancestors *went along* with family and community atrocities, in order to *get along* with those in power.

- Our ancestors reflected a silent indifference in the face of atrocities, and reaped (or raped) the benefits from systems of oppression? Etc.

This list of attitudes and behaviors is not exhaustive in the least, as we might be able to add a few more examples. Yet on the other hand, healing intergenerational trauma means more than just focusing on the negative characteristics that may have been passed down to us. In fact, healing from intergenerational trauma also includes acknowledging our ancestors' resilient, positive characteristics that were passed on as well. From our perspective as the current generation, this awareness of the *other side of the coin* helps form an honest picture of who we are, as well as reinforces a stronger connection we have with our ancestors. For example, in the world of *Positive Psychology*, people are not encouraged to focus on the what is wrong with themselves, but instead, they are encouraged to identify with what positive gifts, graces, skills, and character traits do they already possess? In this way, people are empowered toward a more solution-focused approach to their problems. Another tool I use to help to help people discover their character strengths, comes from Peterson and Seligman (2004) who have identified 24 categories, such as appreciation of beauty, bravery, creativity, curiosity with life, fairness, forgiveness, gratitude, authenticity, etc. As people explore these positive character traits, they are often empowered, perhaps for the first time in their lives, to name what gives their lives meaning and purpose. Yet, this awareness is only the beginning; if we recognize positive character traits in us, chances are that our ancestors may have possessed them too. Remember, trauma is not the only thing that may have been passed down to us. We also have received positive character strengths, strong work ethics, and resiliency to name a few. Either way, to truly live our lives to our greatest potential is also to realize who we are as souls, as well as that our gifts and graces are meant for benefit of others. There are many people who may never realize who they are as souls, let alone, being unable to embrace such strengths in themselves. Perhaps they were never allowed to realize their potentials, or hid these strengths our of fear, rejection or shame. Regardless, positive character traits are in all of us; we just have to find them and reclaim them (Houck, 2014).

Releasing Ourselves, Releasing Others

In bereavement counseling, I always stress to family members that when it comes to their deceased loved-ones, there is no time limit on wanting to say everything they need to say. In other words, it is never too late for an apology, or an expression of love or gratitude, because they are able to hear us. Still, many bereft people feel guilty for not speaking up ahead of time, and now that the loved-one is deceased, they struggle with the *should have, could have* and *would have* missed opportunities to say what they wanted or needed to say. Admittedly, sometimes finding the words to express what and how we are feeling is difficult in the moment, especially if we have never been able to, or even permitted to do so, before. Leading palliative care physician, author, and public advocate Ira Byock (2014), suggests four simple phrases that when spoken, carry enormous power to heal and nurture our interpersonal and intrapersonal relationships: *Please forgive me, I forgive you, thank you,* and *I love you.* Although there is nothing new about uttering these phrases, I believe they are applicable to healing both present and ancestral relationships. To reinforce this concept, I have people look through a kaleidoscope held up to a light. As they see all the shapes and colors of the designs, people often exclaim how beautiful everything appears. Slowly turning the dial, they also see how all the shapes and colors change simultaneously. In fact, as one shape and color changes, it also affects multiple changes in other shapes and colors, and so forth. As they continue to spin the wheel, the smile on their faces tell me that they understand this three-dimensional connectedness. Still, this object lesson is only the beginning and does not quite capture the concept of how our relationships extend beyond time and space. For me, I believe the impact of healing intergenerational trauma can be best understood as a starburst. Much like the sparklers children light on the 4th of July, as one person heals from trauma, the energy radiates out in all directions, time and dimensions. All relationships regardless of time and space are transformed. This is how interconnected we are as human beings and the world in which we live. Just imagine how a single negative thought carries enough destructive energy to affect hundreds, if not thousands, of people each day! Now, imagine that same potential a single positive thought has.

Kayla (pseudo name) was a 15-year-old high school student who was acting out in school. She went from being a *Straight-A* student to getting C's in the course of a semester. As Kayla started experimenting with various drugs, her friends and family noticed significant behavioral changes in her. She became more irritable, hostile and uninterested in normal teenage activities. She was diagnosed with major depression, assessed for suicide ideation and was prescribed anti-depressant medication. Instead of treating her individually, Kayla agreed to family therapy that included her mother and grandmother. At the first meeting, I set the ground rules for therapy, explaining that we were there not to place blame on anyone, but to help Kayla "get better". To get an accurate history of the family, I started drawing a genogram (*a visual representation of a multigenerational family tree that highlights relationships among family members*) on an dry-erase board I had in my office. As the names of cousins, aunts, uncles, and significant family events filled the board, I explained how emotional and behavioral patterns are not only mirrored, but also handed down through the generations. Immediately, metaphorical dots started to connect for Kayla and her mother as stories from Kayla's grandmother filled in the details from her perspective. She explained how she was raise by her mother and grandmother; what it was like growing up in *her day*. She shared how men and women were treated differently, lived with different social and religious expectations, and why jobs were scarce at times. She also shared why so and so had extra-marital affairs, who struggled with excessive drinking and even the reason why a certain family had to move away. All of a sudden, there were now five generations in the room with us, as it appeared that the ground rules for therapy gave Kayla's grandmother permission to talk about the family secrets. Interestingly, every now and then I noticed how Kayla's body language went from sitting with her head in her hands, to carefully listening to her grandmother's stories. I could see in Kayla's eyes that she was starting to understand that she was not crazy, lazy, ugly or stupid, or any other negative belief she told herself.

As we talked over the next few weeks, the genogram depicted generations of socio-economic struggles, alcohol dependence, family attitudes around guilt and shame, and grandma's one big secret: her abortion at age 19. Through her tears, Grandma confessed that she had been carrying the guilt and shame of her abortion for decades. In fact, every now and then, she said how she could hear her baby's cries in her dreams. Although abortion was illegal back in her day, Grandma said she had the abortion anyway, in order to spare her family shame at that time having a child out of wedlock. She also shared how she wanted to tell her husband many times, but still feared being shunned. Immediately, Kayla burst into tears as she too confessed that before last semester she became pregnant and had an abortion. She too could not bear shaming the family with this unplanned pregnancy, since they had so many high hopes for her. All at once, the emotional floodgates were opened as three generations of women sat there and sobbed in each other's arms. The relief from carrying these secrets was palpable in both grandmother and granddaughter. Although Kayla's mother had no idea of these secrets, she too realized that for generations who did not believe in *airing dirty laundry,* suffering in silence is a horrible burden to bear. In the weeks that followed, Kayla, her mother and grandmother continued to talk through generational struggles and unspoken lessons that characterized their family. Kayla and her grandmother even wrote letters of forgiveness to the children they aborted. Grandma also brought in some old photos which added flesh, blood and soul to the stories. Themes of *forgive me, I forgive you, thank you* and *I love you* continued to empower these women to not only heal generations long since passed, but also to impart their hopes and dreams for generations yet to be born.

Opening the Heart: Forgiveness and Gratitude

Healing ourselves and healing our ancestors appears to be, on the surface, a *chicken-egg* dilemma. Who do you heal first? Is it in healing ourselves that we also heal our ancestors, or as we heal our ancestors, do we also heal ourselves? As was seen in Kayla's family, healing occurred simultaneously because of the blood and soul connection the women recognized in each other, as well as beyond each other. Family Systems theorist, Murray Bowen (1993) suggests that a person cannot be fully understood in isolation, i.e., apart from the greater context of one's family, community, culture and the world. However, within these larger systems, people struggle to *differentiate* themselves and to be guided by their own thoughts, feelings and actions. In other words, although individuals desire to think and live for themselves (e.g., developing creative and critical thinking skills), they are often drawn back into the prevailing, and often co-dependent, emotional patterns that characterize families, cultures, societies, etc. Therefore, systems in general are not disregarded, but rather they provide a context from which people define, and at times, redefine, who they are. In order to work through this process of differentiation, Bowen noted that families need to recognize how their present characteristics tend to mirror the intergenerational dysfunction that is a result of unresolved trauma. Characteristics such as marital conflict, dysfunction in one spouse, emotional distance and/or impairment in one or more children, lack of communication, addictions, etc., often mirrors society's anxiety and instability from experiencing wars, genocide, scarcity of natural resources, etc. Again, if the greater systems context of societal dysfunction is addressed, people are better equipped to identify where they need to heal their family system, and vice versa.

Still, if we are honest with ourselves, we may live in a part of the world where society's definition of differentiation is a mixed message: On one hand, differentiation is often taken to the extreme as we are told to look out for number one, be an individual, and walk to the beat of our own drum…even at the expense of others if necessary. Yet on the other hand, there are times when we are also expected to go with the flow, don't make waves, and fall in line with the status quo. If these mixed messages are confusing, we are not alone. All we have to do is examine the history of systems in order to understand the violent and oppressive patterns against people who do not conform to such wishes (Haught, 2002; Black, 2012). When thinking of ancestral healing, we might be hesitant to begin this process because we may still hold a tremendous amount of bitterness, rage and contempt against those who committed physical, emotional or sexual abuse against us or our families. In fact, as we flip through our family albums, we may discover they are not always filled with pleasant memories. Instead, the pages may be filled with more memories of abuse, control, oppression and cruelty. Nevertheless, when we realize that we can be the transitional generation that no longer has to carry such wounds, then our ancestors no longer have to carry them either. Indeed, we all possess inner strengths, resources and gifts to make this happen. Wounded people, wound people. Intergenerational trauma attests to this. However, people who live their lives in forgiveness, gratitude and love, transform generations. Discovering the power of our soul's voice is tremendous catalyst for change.

As previously mentioned, healing intergenerational trauma carries with it a great deal of courage and responsibility because we could just as easily dismiss its importance, and passively accept the world in which we live. However, the dysfunction of social, political, religious, educational, and financial systems of various degrees have not only been handed down to us, but also often serve to reinforce our distorted perceptions of each other. These distortions in systems are so intertwined that it appears nothing happens in a vacuum; all have had a hand in creating and sustaining oppression, coercion and corruption down through the centuries. When we embrace our soul consciousness and transcend towards the realization of who we truly are, we are unable to perpetuate the dysfunction that holds a distorted way of life together. Indeed, the intrapersonal and interpersonal transformation is that powerful. Yet, it is worth noting that just like in family systems, societal systems typically do not tolerate people who are not willing to maintain the status quo. In fact, once a system becomes powerful, members will devalue, dismiss and destroy others in order to hang onto their power. In other words, dysfunctional systems, and the people involved, simply cannot risk being authentic because that makes them vulnerable to the truth, which calls for change in attitudes and behaviors.

The Seven Generations

These days, obtaining ancestral information is made easier with the assistance of on-line searches. In working with intergenerational trauma and ancestral healing, I encourage people to work with three to four generations to start. Ideally, going back seven generations creates a more thorough context for healing to occur, because it is based on the 7th *Generational Principle* originating from the Native American Iroquois Nation (Bear Heart and Larkin, 1998). The Principle taught that every decision, albeit individual or societal, must consider the impact on the seventh generation:

> *The thickness of your skin shall be seven spans —*
> *which is to say that you shall be proof against anger,*
> *offensive actions and criticism. Your heart shall be*
> *filled with peace and good will and your mind filled*
> *with a yearning for the welfare of the people of the*
> *Confederacy. With endless patience you shall carry out*
> *your duty and your firmness shall be tempered with*
> *tenderness for your people. Neither anger nor fury shall*

James A. Houck, Jr., Ph.D.

find lodgement in your mind and all your words and actions shall be marked with calm deliberation. In all of your deliberations in the Confederate Council, in your efforts at law making, in all your official acts, self-interest shall be cast into oblivion. Cast not over your shoulder behind you the warnings of the nephews and nieces should they chide you for any error or wrong you may do, but return to the way of the Great Law which is just and right. Look and listen for the welfare of the whole people and have always in view not only the present but also the coming generations, even those whose faces are yet beneath the surface of the ground — the unborn of the future Nation.

Although the Principle emphasizes the effect present decisions have on seven generations into the future, I believe it also provides us a social context to be able to heal seven generations before us, whose decisions affect us today. For example, every new generation begins approximately between 25-30 years. This means the seventh generation of our ancestors would have begun approximately 175-210 years ago. Therefore, let's say if a person was born in 1980, his/her ancestral context map would look like this:

- 1st generation: 1955-1950   Parents
- 2nd generation: 1930-1920   Great Grandparents
- 3rd generation: 1905-1890   Great, Great Grandparents
- 4th generation: 1880-1860   Etc...
- 5th generation: 1855-1830
- 6th generation: 1830-1800
- 7th generation: 1805-1770

The reason why this social/historical time frame is essential, is because although personal information on our ancestors may be scarce, we can perhaps better understand the times in which they lived:

- What was the majority of norms, social attitudes and/or prejudices at the time?
- What natural disasters or catastrophes would they have faced?
- What were a week's wages and the cost of certain foods, housing?
- What was the nation/state's attitude toward education?
- What wars may have been fought? How might our ancestors been involved?
- What role did religion/spirituality play in people's lives?
- Were there any significant historical traumatic events?
- What social roles would men and women have been forced into?
- How was government viewed at that time? Who was the president? Were there any major laws enacted?
- What were the attitudes toward childrearing?
- What were some of the illnesses and diseases people feared contracting?
- How was death talked about and/or treated in the home and society?
- Etc.

A Return to Clymer

One thing I have learned is that soul healing and release is not just the work of a select few, but all people have the potential to heal their own ancestral relationships. I meet so many people who want to stop the cycle of intergenerational trauma, but are just at a loss as to what they can do. Nevertheless, the best place to begin the journey toward healing is to first examine their own symptoms and situations in life; problems that they struggle with time and time again that they just can't get a handle on. For me, what began on a mass scale of releasing land and the souls held by intergenerational trauma at Montauk, Long Island, was also achieved on an individual basis in working with my family of origin. In my life, it was a struggle with anxiety, but as I probed deeper, I became aware of my unconscious fear of being trapped and suffocating.

For example, for months I knew I had to return to the abandoned mine where over 40+ coal miners were killed in a horrific gas explosion. This was also the place where my grandfather had died from a falling rock as he was mining some 12 years later. As previously mentioned, my father was two years old at the time, and grew up without his father. When I stood at the mouth of the now demolished mine entrance, I drummed quietly and offered tobacco prayers for these men, their families and the surrounding towns. I felt the traumatic pain and heaviness that the land held, as well as the emotional burdens generations of families from other coal mine accidents carried for so long. Ironically, although I was seeking healing for myself, little did I realize that there's going to be healing for many, many others. I asked for forgiveness for the bitterness and any other negative emotion I harbored in my soul against my grandfather and father. In that moment, I realized that perhaps my father was simply incapable of meeting my emotional needs as a parent because his father was not there to meet his emotional needs. His father's death may have also contributed significantly to my father being a very quiet, reserved and anxious man. In fact, all of his life, my father struggled with the attitude that there was/ is something that could always go wrong. He could never put his finger on it, but always felt this free-floating anxiety of impending doom.

Entrance to the abandoned mine
Clymer, PA

I also asked for *forgiveness* for the negativity and bitterness I was holding onto regarding the effect of this trauma had on the family, as well as the fact that nobody talked to me about this trauma as a child. Perhaps they were too overwhelmed to put into words their memories of that day because they were stuck in their own trauma. Furthermore, I also *thanked* my grandfather for his hard work and sacrifice. Perhaps he did not have a choice but to work in the mine. After all, coal mining was the mainstay of communities back then. Perhaps his mother and father struggled with their own emotional pain, knowing that their son was going to work in the same mine that 14 years earlier, was the site of this horrific explosion that killed 40 men. Nevertheless, I thanked him for his dedication, especially when his body ached and the times that he did not feel like going to work. I thanked him for coming home each night to his family, scrubbing up before dinner and watching the coal dirt being rinsed from his hands and body. I thanked him for what he did day in and day out, because people like him and others working in the mines, provided for and sustained the economic energy at that time. And finally, I said that *I loved him*, and even though I never met him, I was honored to be his grandson. Although not a coalminer myself, I could sense the metaphorical coal dust in my veins. I laughed to myself as I remembered the times as a boy I would always dig in the dirt, return home, and was ordered by my mother to take a bath before dinner.

When I finished drumming and praying, I saw my grandfather come up out of the mouth of the mine, dressed in his work clothes and helmet; covered in soot and holding his lunch pail. As I caught a glimpse of him, he immediately was taken up to heaven. To my surprise, other coal miners followed. One by one, those who had died in other mines were being released as well. They climbed out, brushed off the excess soot from their bodies, and then were whisked away to heaven. To me, it seemed as though hundreds of souls, perhaps from other coal mine accidents, came up out of this portal. My soul swelled with joy as I sat there quietly watching these men being transported to heaven. Sometimes, I would resume drumming softly. Once the last coalminer was transported to heaven, I sensed wave after wave of an incredible peace wash over me. The traumatic energy of the land had indeed shifted, and I breathed in a freshness of love, life and light. Interestingly, as I was driving back on the highway, sipping my coffee, and trying to fathom everything that had taken place when all of a sudden, images flashed before my eyes. I saw my grandfather, still dressed in his work clothes, and my father as an adult, standing arm in arm, smiling and laughing, reunited once again.

In the day and weeks that followed this ancestral healing, I continued to process this history of my grandfather and father through dreams and journaling. However, what I remembered most about that day when the souls of the coalminers were released, was the immediate lessening of my anxious feelings. No longer did I have this feeling of a free-floating, impending doom, cloud over my head. The negative psychological, emotional, and spiritual energy that the mine once held for me, and hundreds of others, had been transformed into a peaceful resiliency of grace. I will always have this family history to tell, but now I tell the story from a healthier perspective.

Healing Your Ancestors, Healing Your Path

Before beginning any ancestral healing, please consider your motivation. Creating a dialogue with our ancestors is not a game, nor is it to be taken lightly. However, many people find a richness that comes into their lives, knowing their ancestors exist beyond the limits of time and space. Indeed, our ancestors are very much a part of our lives, whether or not we realize it. In fact, every time we visit a loved-one's gravesite, or remember them in other ways, we carry on an internal dialogue with them in the conversations or experiences we had. Every anniversary, birthday or other special occasions, remind us that our relationships continue to exist beyond the grave. In these cases, we are reminded that some family issues have been resolved; others have not. Still, their voices of pain, suffering and perhaps trauma have brought us to this moment in which we are now ready to embrace the implications of our family healing. So, let's begin.

Find a quiet place where you will not be disturbed. Photographs or images of ancestors are a great way to recreate visual cues and should be included in this healing process. If this is your first time doing ancestral healing, I would recommend you set your intention to work with only your parents, grandparents and/or great grandparents. Turn off all cell phones and make sure you will not be disturbed. Center your soul through prayer and meditation. Set your intention to consciously connect with your ancestors and offer healing for those who need to be released from being stuck in their trauma. At this point, it is also wise to set your intention to be released from any psychological, emotional and/or spiritual wounds that you carry unconsciously. Be honest with yourself about any known offenses that you are not ready to forgive. At the same time, ask God for the grace needed to recognize if there are any underlying misperceptions about your ancestors or their effect on you. Other questions to consider include:

- What were the lessons, rules and values that you were taught as a child?
- Who taught you such lessons?
- Which lessons do you agree with? Which ones have you discarded?
- How have family secrets benefitted and burdened the family?
- Which memories of your loved ones no longer serve you? Which ones still do?
- What physical/emotional/psychological/spiritual wounds do you need to forgive, let go of or be released from?
- Which of these wounds do you believe you need to hold onto, and why?
- What is the internal message these wounds say to you about you?
- What promises did you ever make to your loved-ones that you might need to be forgiven for not keeping?
- What have you been thankful for in your family? How was/is it expressed?
- When was the last time your family/ancestors told you they loved you?
- When was the last time you told your family/ancestors you loved them?
- What other family stories do you remember?

The following is a contextual narrative I use with my ancestors. You are free to adapt the wording as it suits your situation. When it is appropriate, be sure to include the themes of forgiveness, gratitude and love. Some people find healing with their ancestors immediately; others will find that their healing involves more of a process. At any rate, you can return again and again when you feel the need to heal, be reconciled with others, or express gratitude. Regardless, note how you feel before, during and after. Journal your experiences and pay attention to your dreams. If at any time you feel overwhelmed by unpleasant memories, you may stop and return to this dialogue at a later time. Some people also incorporate this exercise into their personal therapy for extra processing.

When you are ready, close your eyes and imagine yourself in a large, open area. In front of you there are thousands of people; some of their faces you can recognize and some you cannot. These are your ancestors, your relatives, your kin. Begin the conversation by saying: *this is your grandson/granddaughter and I am here to help heal our family. I have heard your cries and recognize your voices in the things I have struggled and/or suffered with. Your physical, psychological, emotional and spiritual pain is my pain, and my pain is your pain. Yet, your physical, psychological, emotional and spiritual joy is also my joy, and my joy is also your joy. When I have looked at my life, I have become _____ at times with what I have struggled with, and what has been passed down to me. I ask your forgiveness and release, for not fully understanding your struggles, pain, and suffering. I do not want to carry this burden any longer.*

At that time, ask if there are any ancestors who need to be forgiven for what they have done during their lifetime, so they can be healed and released from the trauma that has weighed them down. One or two may step forward, or groups may come forward, depending on whether the forgiveness is a shared burden. If you are centering on one or two relatives, address them by name. Look at them with compassion and realize the historical context in which they lived. Say, *I forgive you for what you have done, and I no longer carry this burden. Therefore, be released from your burdens and be set free, no longer bound by your traumatic experiences, as well as any guilt and shame that has trapped you for so long. I also thank you for the blessings you have given me; the positive characteristics in my life* (name them) *and I am grateful. And thank you for your perseverance, because I am here today.* There may also be ancestors that come forward at that time and offer their own gratitude for being forgiven and released from their trauma and burdens. Repeat this conversation as long as it is necessary. A sense of peace may fill you when you realize it is time to close. Finally, say *I love you and I am grateful for being part of this family. Be released to go with God.* To close this time with your ancestors, offer a prayer, mantra or other positive meditation to reinforce the healing that has taken place. Some people say the Lord's Prayer, Moola Mantra, or sing a Native American Indian ancestral song, Irish blessing, or another favorite prayer or hymn. In my family, it is traditional to read *Gone From My Sight* by Henry Van Dyke (1852-1933) at every graveside ceremony. I often use this poem as a meditation when I finish an ancestral healing:

> *I am standing upon the seashore. A ship, at my side, spreads her white sails to the moving breeze and starts for the blue ocean. She is an object of beauty and strength. I stand and watch her until, at length, she hangs like a speck of white cloud just where the sea and sky come to mingle with each other. Then, someone at my side says, 'There, she is gone' Gone where? Gone from my sight. That is all. She is just as large in mast, hull and spar as she was when she left my side. And, she is just as able to bear her load of living freight to her destined port. Her diminished size is in me - not in her. And, just at the moment when someone says, 'There, she is gone,' there are other eyes watching her coming, and other voices ready to take up the glad shout, 'Here she comes!'*

For the next few days, be particularly mindful to journal any insights, impressions or dreams that arise. Also, make note of any changes in your perspectives regarding your present relationships. How do you now view yourself and others? In what ways do your now treat yourself and others differently. How do others appear to treat you? In what ways are you more understanding, loving, compassionate, forgiving, and patient with yourself and others? More importantly, have you noticed how you now tell your family stories from a different perspective?

We Are Born Storytellers

This change in how we tell our intergenerational traumatic stories indicates that a transformational healing in relationships has occurred that exceeds time and space. More than just recounting facts, dates and figures, our stories carry with them elements of healing, grace and hope for all of humanity. In other words, story-telling has always been a key piece in sustaining cultural and generational identity, as people tell their stories as a means of preserving memories of loved-ones, as well as reinforcing a sense of personal uniqueness. In counseling others struggling with intergenerational trauma, I have noticed that when people have not been able to transform the negative energy around tragic events, their stories are told the same each time...every time. As a boy, I remember listening to the same family stories at picnics, holidays and other family gatherings. I heard these accounts so often, that by the time I was a teenager, I could recite them word for word. Now with the benefit of hindsight, I also understand that not only did these details not change, but also the story-tellers' interpretation and attitudes remained the same. In fact, there was always an underlying tone of helplessness, bitterness, sadness, and resentment that drove how the story was told. Ironically, it was almost as if the story was not being told *correctly* if these negative emotions were absent.

From the time when we are born, our understanding of the world is placed within a story. From being read bedtime stories or reading books, to watching shows and listening to others, stories provided us the context, and mental images, for making sense of life. Austrian born physician, psychotherapist and pioneer of individual psychology, Alfred Adler (1870-1937) believed that stories not only provided form to our earliest memories, but also these stories became the blueprint for how we live our lives in relation to others. Perhaps one reason why our psychological, emotional and spiritual healing is so elusive then, is due to the misperception that we believe we are separate from our problems (Adler and Brett, 2009). For example, part of healing from intergenerational trauma not only involves telling our stories, but also involves reclaiming our empowerment to rewrite our stories that are now life-empowering and affirming. We do not achieve this empowerment from an embellished, delusional view that nicely ties up stories in a bow. Instead, our stories are now told from a healthier perspective; a place from one's healing. Granted, we may not be able to recall every experience, but for those moments that stand out to us, they serve as our *unconscious logic* about how we see ourselves, our relationship with others, and the motivation for our behavior today. For example, a useful tool for understanding how our personal healing mirrors our story-telling perspectives can be seen in the Adlerian *Life Style Assessment* (Ibid). Among other accounts of our birth order and family constellation, this *Assessment* includes recalling our earliest memories. People typically recall two or three earliest memories, one memory from later childhood, one memory from adolescence, and then one memory from early adulthood. From each of these memories, people tell or journal their stories with as much detail as they can remember. Then after each memory, they complete the following open-ended phrases from the perspective of how old they were in the story:

I am _____

Others are _____

The world is_____

Therefore, I will _____

For instance, an adult sharing an earliest memory from a birthday party at age 4, might remember how disappointed she felt when her favorite aunt was not there to watch her blow out the candles on the cake. From the perspective of that 4-year-old, she might complete these phrases this way: _I am sad... others are singing... the world is noisy... and therefore I will blow out my candles._ Other subsequent memories from the person might then follow a similar interpretation of experiences that form the person's behavioral pattern as seen through her eyes of a later child, adolescent, and early adult: _Since others don't seem to notice/care how I feel, I will go along with others and do what they want me to do._ However, as these perspectives of insignificance and unworthiness are healed and transformed as an adult, the interpretation of recalling these earliest memories change into a healthier story-telling. Returning to the memory of the birthday party, the 4-year-old did not realize at the time that her aunt was unable to see her blow out her candles, not because she did not care, but because she stopped to help another person involved in a car accident (and was holding pressure on a deep cut until the ambulance arrived). However, the earliest memory of that birthday party was internalized at a young age as _I am not important, so I have to ignore my feelings and go along with the crowd._ Now, when the adult has healed from this negative self-talk, a healthier perspective is integrated into her earliest memory. As a result, the adult can still recall the birthday party. However, not only does she tell the story differently based on a more thorough picture of _when, where, how_ and _with whom_ these early beliefs developed, but also her present relationships are healthier. For example,

> _I am sad, but although my favorite aunt was not there to see me blow out my candles, I understand now that she needed to help someone else..._

> *Others are singing, because they did not know what happened to my aunt, and not that they were insensitive to my feelings…*
>
> *The world is noisy, and sometimes dangerous, but thank God there are people who stop to help others in need…*
>
> *Therefore, I will also do what I need to do in the moment without dismissing my feelings. I still got a hug and a kiss from my aunt, and so did that injured person from the car accident. She saved a life that day! By the way…did I tell you that it was because of my aunt that I went into nursing?*

This healthier perspective often forms in people a greater sense of identity, as well as a deeper sense of compassion, empathy and grace towards others. Healing from intergenerational trauma also has this same affect. When healing occurs within the greater context of generations, people tell their stories much differently from a healthier, more holistic perspective. The reason why we can tell our stories differently is because much of the healing involves becoming aware of the former, negative perceptions and self-talk that no longer serve us. In other words, we recognize how these cognitive schemas have been draining our energy, distorting our perceptions, and diminishing our potential for healthier relationships. In fact, when we replace these with more transformative and life-giving perspectives, the starburst of energy heals all generations across time and space.

> *You can tell your story from the place where it no longer dominates you. You can speak about it with a certain distance and see it as the way to your present freedom.*
>
> Henri Nouwen (1999)

Creating a Living Dialogue With One's Ancestors

*The tragedy of life is not death, but what we let die inside
ourselves as we live.*

Native American Indian proverb

In creating a living dialogue with one's ancestors, remember that
our soul connection with them is not about placing blame or finding
fault for wounds suffered from intergenerational trauma. Instead, it
is a dialogue intended to create an on-going opportunity for healing
and reconciliation, as well as stopping the harmful psychological,
emotional and spiritual patterns from being passed on to generations
yet to be born. Being the transitional generation therefore, requires
us to *stand in the gap* as it were, and offer release not just for ourselves,
but also for all family members regardless of whether or not they
were perpetrators or victims. For example, I have friends who set
their intention to heal intergenerational trauma from the perspective
of the unborn generations. Much like going back seven generations
to heal souls that are stuck due to trauma, they place themselves
in the role/voice of seven generations in the future. Returning to
the example of a person who was born in 1980, the effect of healing
intergeneration trauma (or not) would then impact generations up to
the approximate year 2145. From this perspective, the need of healing
intergenerational trauma now is crucial if the next seven generations
are to be empowered to begin their life on earth free from traumatic
baggage and needless family suffering.

- 1st generation: 1980   Parent
- 2nd generation: 2005   Children
- 3rd generation: 2045   Grandchildren
- 4th generation: 2070   Great Grandchildren
- 5th generation: 2095   Great, Great Grandchildren
- 6th generation: 2120   Etc.
- 7th generation: 2145

Still, many people ask me: *How do you heal intergenerational trauma when you do not even know your present family, let alone connect with ancestors and those who have yet to be born?* The answer is that religious and social ceremonies/rituals bring us back into a *spiritual, psychological, emotional* and *physical* alignment, or awareness, with God, ourselves, and our relations. No matter what nationality, race, ethnicity, or region we are from, every culture has their own unique celebrations. Many ceremonies mark transitions in our lives such as graduations, weddings and funerals. Others are more seasonal and follow a yearly observance, e.g., birthdays, anniversaries, holidays, solstice celebrations, etc. Regardless of when a particular ceremony is observed, or whether or not people are connected to their community, there are always universal teachings, often hidden in the rituals, that can be applied to all of humanity.

> *The purpose of religion should be to help us maintain a binding commitment to spiritual awareness within the lives of our communities. This is done through the power of ritual, which is the materialization of religion, the bearer of religious tradition, the insurer of continuity of the life of the present with the original spirit of the past. The re-enactment of traditional ritual in worship by provided by religion ensures that the past (our ancestors) continues to touch our bodies, our flesh, and to reach into the hearts of our souls* (Mehl-Madrona, 2010).

For example, every August the village of Picuris Pueblo in New Mexico holds their Harvest Festival. During the celebration there are endless ceremonies commemorating the connection the people have with God the Creator and Sustainer of life, the abundance from the land, and the love of their community. There are religious services, foot races, indigenous drumming, singing, dances and of course, sharing meals together. The first time I attended this celebration, I was struck by the large 25-30-foot wooden pole erected in the middle of the town. On top of this pole were tied a sheep's carcass, a blanket and a watermelon. The elders explained to me that these items symbolized God's provision of food, clothing and connection to the land. The culmination of the Festival involved retrieval of these items by dancer clowns dressed in black and white. Apart from reminding the people of the importance of laughter and play as they worked their way through the crowds, it was the main responsibility of these clowns to climb the pole and recover the items. In good comic fashion, the clowns would make several valiant efforts to climb the pole (e.g., swinging from ropes, standing on each other's shoulders, sliding down, etc.) much to the amusement and encouragement of the crowd. Finally, after several attempts one clown would reach the top as cheers erupted from the crowd below. One by one the items would be lowered and received with joy. As I sat there watching, I was reminded of the teaching that surrounded this ceremony: *Unless the clowns retrieved these items each year, the people would die* (Rael, 2012). Initially, I thought this teaching was strange. After all, the community could not live off of exclusively a watermelon, a sheep and a blanket. Then finally the meaning of the ceremony hit me: Failure to retrieve these items was not meant to be taken as a literal death, but rather it is *what dies within the people as they live* is what matters most. Apart from food, clothing, and shelter, the real issues that we cannot afford to live without are hope, love, gratitude, inner peace and grace. These virtues are the true life-giving gifts that nourish and sustain the soul that far exceeds material possessions. Because ceremonies and rituals contain deeper levels of meaning, succeeding generations need to learn the relevance ceremonies have for them to live in their soul consciousness. By doing so, nothing is taken for granted in this life; not one breath, one sip of water nor one opportunity to bring healing from trauma in another's life. Everything and everyone is connected.

CHAPTER EIGHT

Living As Souls

In the depths of your being there is an inner peace that is experienced when the truth of who you really are is unveiled.

Swami Paramanand Ji Mahraj

When we begin listening to the cries of our ancestors, becoming more aware of our own soul's voice is inevitable, and vice versa. As our soul consciousness matures, we realize that we share an eternal connectedness with all creation that exceeds our present time and space. Although this initial awakening is often met with excitement and joy, we are often faced with recurring questions such as, *Now what? What is expected of me? How do I live out this awareness each day? Etc.?* Indeed, these are all good questions, ones in which we will spend the rest of our lives answering. In fact, a continual awareness of our soul consciousness and connection, enables significant emotional, psychological and spiritual shifts is us. In fact, we no longer can see things the way we used to, because our perceptions have undergone a wonderful transformation as our inner awakening challenges us to live more authentic lives. Moreover, inner transformation compels us to not only re-think and re-evaluate our former ways, but also compels us to transcend, or go beyond, our perceived personal limitations.

Let's begin with a simple question: *How differently would we live our lives if we fully realized ourselves as souls?* The answer is that our lives would look a lot different than what they appear to be at the present moment. I also suspect that we would be so empowered to treat ourselves, and all relationships, with the fullest extent of kindness, love, patience, compassion and grace, that the world would then definitely sit up and take notice. When I was in graduate school, I was first exposed to Abraham Maslow's *Hierarchy of Needs* as a means of understanding our human nature and striving to achieve personal goals. This model of understanding the self follows the logic that our lives go through stages of attaining personal needs, i.e., food, clothing, shelter, security, intimacy with others, goals, life meaning and purpose, etc. (Maslow, 2014). Ironically, many people today believe that once they attain self-actualization, or discovering their life's purpose, motivation and meaning, then they will have finally found their life satisfaction that has long so eluded them. However, many are often met with a harsh reminder that in attaining one's dreams, ambitions and goals, does not necessarily guarantee happiness, let alone finding this inner peace. Moreover, despite their accomplishments, people still sense something is missing from their lives. If this is so, why then, do so many people feel empty when they have so much? What is the problem? Perhaps these feelings of disappointment with Maslow's *Hierarchy* stems from a misperception that it is a flawed model. Perhaps we need to understand that this model is *limited*. Self-actualization carries us only so far.

Attaining true happiness, joy and peace in our lives comes not in the accumulation of things, degrees and accomplishments, but rather these come from the grace of God's presence that can only touch our soul. Indeed, there is a greater depth of contentment, forgiveness, love, joy, peace, etc., that awakens in us when we fully realize ourselves as souls. And, it is through God's grace that we are able to recognize our soul's connection to God and throw off the cloak of illusion. Still, the limitation of Maslow's model does not mean that self-actualization is a worthless pursuit. On the contrary, we all need to have our basic physical needs met, a sense of personal security, meaningful relationships and attainable goals in our lives. However, we must also understand that these earthly pursuits are always pointing us towards a higher awakening of self-realization of who we truly are.

Interestingly, we can learn this lesson as we become involved in healing intergenerational trauma. However, the first thing we need to do is to first step outside our linear thinking of past, present and future, take a leap of faith, and fall into God's grace that opens us up to this expanded consciousness. Once we realize who we are, we are then empowered to reengage Maslow's *Hierarchy* from a more life-giving inspiration that focuses not on an ego-driven achievement, but rather that which enhances the value, dignity and worth of all relationships. For example, realized souls are no longer motivated to feed others just for the sake of alleviating their own guilt and filling empty stomachs, but rather their motivation comes from the awareness that by feeding others, they are also feeding souls with compassion and grace. Instead of spending time with another out of obligation, realized souls instead see another soul in need of friendship and love. Instead of forgiving others from the perspective of *what do we get out of it*, we instead forgive because we will not allow people to carry the crippling effects un-forgiveness and bitterness has on them, and us, as souls. All in all, as we bless others in the physical sense, we also bless them in the spiritual sense. In fact, when we meet the basic needs in others, these benevolent acts inevitably nudge them closer to discover who they authentically are as soul. Never diminish even the simplest acts of kindness, compassion and grace, for these are truly the acts that touch the soul and cause all of heaven to rejoice. Even a cup of cold water can invoke this (Matthew 10:42). Self-realization fulfills self-actualization.

Hearing the Cries of the Weak and Wounded

Listening to the cries of our ancestors compels us to heal our relationships with them, as well as begin to interact with all people on a soul-level. Yet, is self-realization powerful enough to transform social systems that promote oppression, prejudice and control? Many people would say that the more we understand the history of humanity, transforming systems is impossible. In fact, there are some who consider systems to be suspect in and of themselves, and therefore choose to work outside the system. Then, there are some people who choose to remain within the system and work with individuals to create change. Whichever your preference, we can say for certain that self-realization transforms *people*, from an ego-driven consciousness to a soul consciousness, which in turn, has an impact on systems. One day, a former student of mine reminded me of this potential effect by saying that *we ought never allow the coldness of an institution to discourage us from finding the warmth of individuals*. This is a very profound statement. Indeed, the more we embrace the fact that all persons are souls, the more awakened we are to change the world. Although we can understand the historical impact of governmental, educational, religious and other social systems, it is their dysfunctional interconnectedness that often reinforces contemporary negative behaviors of oppression, prejudice and abuse of power. But if we truly believe we can create a lasting change in ourselves, others, and the world, then we must admit that transformation is difficult (not impossible) to achieve within present, dysfunctional systems that resist change. For example, dysfunctional systems perpetuate intergenerational trauma because they typically distort the message of *what they believe* endows humanity with its value, dignity and worth. Furthermore, humanity's motivations and behaviors are inaccurately assessed, perhaps along the lines of productivity and consumerism, over and against placing value on a person as soul. Unfortunately, if the dysfunction, or illusion, is never addressed, healed, and removed, then the ramifications of these attitudes and behaviors affect generation, after generation, after generation. Some present systems have been broken and dysfunctional for many generations; if they do not change, they will continue to deteriorate. However, transformation is always possible because systems are made up of individuals. Indeed, their dysfunction in inter/intrapersonal relationships will always come to light because their thoughts, speech and behavior arise out of their emotional, psychological and/or spiritual wounds. Moreover, such wounds hinder people from awakening to who they truly are and therefore, remain unable to embrace their soul consciousness. This inability is not a fault issue or character flaw, but it just might be where they are on their life path; a path that can be liberated towards self-realization at any given moment.

Throughout the centuries, shame and guilt have often been used in our society as a means to control people, i.e., to shame them into feeling a certain way about themselves, and/or make people feel guilty in order to get them to do something. Unfortunately, society has, on more than one occasion, interchanged these words to convey its disappointment in others. For example, people often hear *shame on you*, or *you ought to be ashamed of yourself!* Immediately, there is a sense that something is wrong, and someone is disappointed. With shame, people internalize that message to mean...*there's something wrong with me*, or *I am flawed in some way. I don't measure up to another's expectations of how they see me.* Guilt, on the other hand, is not necessarily a negative feeling. It does communicate to us that we did something wrong, and perhaps go back and fix the error, or ask forgiveness, etc. In this context, guilt also has the potential to be healing and life-giving in relationships. However, guilt can also be manipulated by some to coerce others to do what they want them to do. We might hear certain phrases like, *after all I've done for you*, or *even so and so thinks this about you.* However, shame and guilt, as well as stereotypes, prejudices, sexism, classism, racism, etc. can find no place in the language of the soul. Once we become firmly rooted in our soul consciousness, manipulation in the form of shame and guilt no longer affect us. Therefore, in this one example, the more we see ourselves and others as souls, the more we are able to transform and transcend beliefs that no longer serve us. When this awareness occurs, not only do our relationships take on a healthier tone that transcend time and space, but also, we also understand the futility of waiting for systems to change. They simply cannot do this on their own. British author David Icke (1999) states that *if you are fighting the system, then you're still caught in it. It's not about fighting the system; it's about ceasing to hold it together.*

We are all beautiful souls made in the image of God, full of inherent value, dignity and worth. Yet, we may struggle to accept this truth because our attention is often diverted to focus solely on outward appearances and behaviors. In other words, we all live with some degree of ignorance of our soul consciousness. We may get glimpses of it, but never attain the full extent, because physical, emotional and psychological issues cloud our vision of who we truly are. For example, diseases and illnesses do afflict us in the body. We do feel physical and emotional pain with so much intensity at times, that we believe they are going to break us in two. At times, our lungs may struggle to take a breath, or hunger and diseases causes our stomach, intestines, bones, muscles and blood to scream in agony. These experiences might make us question whether or not we are the soul whom God has created? However, this illusion lies not in the suffering, pain and agony we experience, but rather, it is in our *perception* that there is nothing more to us than an emotional, intellectual and physical body. Indeed, physical and emotional pain and suffering can temporarily drown out the cry of our soul, but our soul is never silenced. Furthermore, the truth is that the greatest strength of who we are as souls, lies in our ability to transform and transcend physical, emotional and psychological limitations. For as much as history has shown us the horrific crimes humanity does to itself, there are just as many stories of humanity rising above such tragedies to heal and reclaim their soul.

> *There's a long road of suffering ahead of you. But don't lose courage. You've already escaped the gravest danger: selection. So now, muster your strength, and don't lose heart. We shall all see the day of liberation. Have faith in life. Above all else, have faith. Drive out despair, and you will keep death away from yourselves. Hell is not for eternity. And now, a prayer - or rather, a piece of advice: let there be comradeship among you. We are all brothers, and we are all suffering the same fate. The same smoke floats over all our heads. Help one another. It is the only way to survive.*
>
> Elie Wiesel, (2006)

Healing the Disenfranchised

The greatest effect hearing the cries of our ancestors has on us not only comes from getting in touch with our own soul's voice, but also it awakens us to hear the cries of those who have no voice today. There has always existed in society a pattern of disenfranchising the weak and wounded; people who have been labeled as unlovable, untouchable and therefore, unreachable. For some, disenfranchisement was due to their disease or illness. For others it was due to their poverty. Still, for others it was due to their gender, race, religion, politics, or social class. Many in society preferred such people not to be seen, let alone heard from. However, just as the cries of our ancestors, and those who have been the victims of crimes against humanity, can never be silenced, so too are the cries of the disenfranchised heard above the din of everyday life. Their cries are not only heard deep within the soul, but also their pain can be given a voice through those who speak for them.

In the Book of Leviticus, there were specific laws (chapters 11-27) given to the Ancient Israelites that guarded against people taking advantage of the disenfranchised. These laws were referred to as the Holiness Code. The Code served as instructions for the people to maintain their holiness before God and one another. According to these laws, holiness was a condition which permeated all aspects of life. From birth to death, life was governed by maintaining a distinction between the holy and the profane, or between the clean and unclean. As Wenham (1979) notes, *cleanliness* was understood as the normal condition of most things and persons, and therefore, spiritual holiness was symbolized by physical perfection. Anything else, e.g., death, sickness, disease, coming in contact with bodily discharges, blood, etc., was considered a deviation of this norm. When people violated this code directly or indirectly, they were separated for a period of time from the community to avoid further contamination. For example, since the Ancient Israelites were forbidden to come in contact with blood, (because blood contained the life of a person) a woman was considered *ceremonially unclean* each month during her menstruation. This rule also included being separated from the community for a certain amount of time after she had given birth to her child (Leviticus 12:1-8). Depending on whether she gave birth to a son or daughter, also determined the amount of time she not only remained separate from her community, but also how long she was forbidden to touch any sacred objects or enter the sanctuary to worship God. Whatever she touched in her unclean state also became defiled. Likewise, matters of sickness and disease also rendered people ceremonially unclean (Leviticus 13-15). Until the physical conditioned improved, people who suffered infectious diseases were temporarily isolated from their community. Typically, this involved about one week. In this isolated state, just as with the rules that applied to women during their menstruation, any object that came in contact with the infectious person also became unclean and had to be washed or destroyed. If other people touched the unclean object on purpose or by accident, they also became unclean and were required to perform ceremonial washing.

By today's standards some might consider these purity laws, which not only categorized people and objects as clean or unclean, but also banished people from the community, as being extreme. Yet what needs to be emphasized here was that a state of uncleanliness was never meant to be permanent. Although God demanded holiness in everyday life, God never abandoned the people. In fact, provisions were made in these laws for people to be redeemed from their unclean conditions and be welcomed back into the camp. For example, once the person's condition, say from an infectious disease, had returned to normal or enough time had elapsed, the person would be readmitted to the community by having the priest pronounce him/her *clean*, and specific sacrifices were then offered to complete the ritual of purification. Unfortunately, by the time of Jesus' day in the first century C.E., the practice of temporarily quarantining unclean people became an acceptable way to expel them . . . permanently. This behavior was justified by the perception that unclean people somehow polluted the rest of society by their conditions (Black, 1996). Therefore, it was quite common for people who had leprosy to live in their own colony outside a town. To survive they had to beg for food and clothing, all from a distance lest the wind would blow their uncleanliness onto the townsfolk, or a passer-by. This expulsion was true not only for people who had an identifiable condition, but also for those who had a condition that was not readily seen, such as mental illness. Similar to leprosy, mentally ill people were either forced to live in isolation or with like-conditioned people (Houck, 2010). As a result, Jesus took no delight in the systems of his day that labeled, ridiculed and excluded the weak and wounded. Instead, Jesus' ministry was characterized by going beyond the Levitical law and reaching directly into the soul. He saw disenfranchised people oppressed by a system that had gone awry, and therefore not only sought wounded people out, but also healed and brought them back into community:

> *He (Jesus) went to Nazareth, where he had been brought up, and on the Sabbath day he went into the synagogue, as was his custom. He stood up to read, and the scroll of the prophet Isaiah was handed to him. Unrolling it, he found the place where it is written: 'The Spirit of the Lord is on me, because he has anointed me to proclaim good news to the poor. He has sent me to proclaim freedom for the prisoners and recovery of sight for the blind, to set the oppressed free, to proclaim the year of the Lord's favor.' Then he rolled up the scroll, gave it back to the attendant and sat down. The eyes of everyone in the synagogue were fastened on him. He began by saying to them, 'Today this scripture is fulfilled in your hearing.'*
>
> Luke 4:16-21

All in all, the beauty, strength and implications of healing intergenerational trauma can be seen when we fully understand how our present relationships leave no room for stereotypes, prejudices, sexism, classism, ableism, ageism, racism, etc. The soul knows nothing of these things because these *isms* are based solely on external forms, e.g., the color of skin, physical traits, gender, birthplace, etc. In fact, when we consider the mounting evidence of centuries and centuries of intergenerational crimes against humanity, there is a shared *modus operandi* based exclusively on the inability to view others beyond physical and cultural characteristics:

> *The fact is that someone born in the United States is not more special than someone born in Mexico; nor is someone born in England more special than someone born in Peru; nor someone who is white than someone who is black. Go down to the seashore, hold a droplet of water in your hand, and tell me how that droplet can possibly be any more or less special than the billions of droplets you see before you in the ocean.*

(Icke, 1999)

When I was in India (which also struggles with disenfranchised people called *Dalits*) both my Hindu and Sikh gurus and friends encouraged me to think of our soul as a drop of water, and God is the ocean. Since both the droplets and the ocean consist of water (H_2O), there is always a connection. Moreover, as in the form of rain, droplets fall and eventually return to be part of the ocean again. Indeed, water may take many forms from solid to liquid to gas, but the chemical characteristic remains the same. In other words, there is never a time when water droplets are not connected to the ocean (Swami Paramanand Ji, 2007). The same is true with the individual soul and God. Because God is Soul and has created us as souls, we are connected to God and God is connected to us. Christianity also acknowledges this soul connection as the Apostle Paul writes:

> *For I am convinced that neither death nor life, neither angels nor demons, neither the present nor the future, nor any powers, neither height nor depth, nor anything else*

in all creation, will be able to separate us from the love
of God that is in Christ Jesus our Lord.

Romans 8:38

Therefore, healing our ancestors from intergenerational trauma awakens and reinforces this connection. When we awaken to our own soul consciousness, we are also empowered to live out our God connection in human relationships. Each day in India I was reminded of this truth as I was greeted with folded hands, a slight bow, and the gentle expression of *Namaste; the Soul in me bows to the Soul in you.*

Tremendous courage is needed to heal intergenerational trauma, embrace the truth, and transform into the beautiful soul that you are. Whether or not you know much about your ancestral line, and whether or not you see yourself coming from a long history of slaves, slaveowners, oppressors, murderers, healers, victims, blue-collar workers, white-collar workers, victims of addictions or suicide, divorce, or healthy relationships, these all have a physical, emotional, psychological and spiritual component to discovering the truth. Yes, the truth does set us free, but it is a freedom that comes with a tremendous amount of responsibility to continue the soul healing process in the lives of those who have come before us, and those yet to be born. *Mitakuye Oyasin!*

Traditional Lakota Sioux Prayer

Aho Mitakuye Oyasin ...All my relations. I honor you
in this circle of life with me today. I am grateful for this
opportunity to acknowledge you in this prayer....
To the Creator, for the ultimate gift of life, I thank you.
To the mineral nation that has built and maintained my
bones and all foundations of life experience, I thank you.
To the plant nation that sustains my organs and body and
gives me healing herbs for sickness, I thank you.

James A. Houck, Jr., Ph.D.

To the animal nation that feeds me from your own flesh and offers
your loyal companionship in this walk of life, I thank you.
To the human nation that shares my path as a soul upon
the sacred wheel of Earthly life, I thank you.
To the Spirit nation that guides me invisibly through the ups and downs
of life and for carrying the torch of light through the Ages, I thank you.
To the Four Winds of Change and Growth, I thank you.
You are all my relations, my relatives, without whom I would not
live. We are in the circle of life together, co-existing, co-dependent, co-
creating our destiny. One, not more important than the other. One
nation evolving from the other and yet each dependent upon the one
above and the one below. All of us a part of the Great Mystery.
Thank you for this Life.

My Tiwa teacher and me
Mesa, AZ

BIBLIOGRAPHY

Abbot, S. E. (2014). Differentiation. Glossary of educational reform. Retrieved from: http://edglossary.org/differentiation/

Adamson, L., & Frick, J. (2003). The still face: A history of a shared experimental paradigm. *Infancy, 4 (4)*, 451-473.

Adler, A. and Brett, C. (2009). *What life could mean for you: The psychology of personal development, rep rev edition.* Oneworld Publications.

Ainsworth, M., Blehar, M., Waters, E., and Wall, S. (2015). Patterns of attachment: A psychological study of the strange situation. *Psychology Press & Routledge Classic Editions, 1st Edition.*

Ainsworth, M. and Bell, S. (1970). Attachment, exploration, and separation: Illustrated by the behavior of one-year-olds in a strange situation. *Child Development*, 41:49-67.

Alger, A.M. (2014, June 12). I don't know who I am anymore: Losing my identity [Web log post]. Retrieved from: http://www.counselling-directory.org.uk/counsellor-articles/i-dont-know-who-i-am-anymore-losing-my-identity.

American Psychiatric Association. (2013). *Diagnostic and statistical manual of mental disorders, 5th edition.* Washington, DC.

Amstutz, Mark R. (2005). *The healing of nations: The promise and limits of political forgiveness.* Rowman & Littlefield.

Andersen, H.C. (1845). *The snow queen: New fairy tales, first volume.* Second Collection.

Andersson, Rani-Henrik. (2009). *The Lakota ghost dance of 1890.* University of Nebraska Press.

Annett, K. (2006). *Unrepentant: Kevin Annett and Canada's genocide.* 109 minutes.

Annett, K. (2012). Smoking gun document, concealed by Anglican Church, points to planned genocide of Mohawk Nation. Retrieved from: http://itccs.org/2012/07/28/smoking-gun- document-concealed-by-anglican-church-points-to-planned-genocide-of-mohawk-nation/.

Archibald, J. (2008). *Indigenous story-work: Educating the heart, mind, body and spirit.* UBC Press.

Arkell, H. and Michael, N. (2015). Ten mother and baby homes carried out vaccine trials on almost 300 children. Retrieved from: http://www.thejournal.ie/baby-deaths-mother-baby-homes-Jun2014/.

Atkinson, J. (2002). *Trauma trails, recreating song lines: The transgenerational effects of trauma in Indigenous Australia.* North Melbourne: Spinifex Press.

Bailey, L. R. (1986). Gehenna: The topography of hell. *Biblical Archeologist,* 49:187.

Bakiner, O. (2016). *Truth commissions: Memory, power, and legitimacy.* University of Pennsylvania Press.

Banai, E., Mikulincer, M. and Shaver, P. (2005). Self-object needs in Kohut's self-psychology: Self-cohesion, affect regulation, and adjustment. *Psychoanalytic Psychology*, 22, (2): 224-260.

Banning, C. (1946). Food shortage and public health: First half of 1945. *Annals of the American*. Sage Journals.

Bear Heart, Larkin, M. (1998). *The wind is my mother: The life and teachings of a Native American shaman*. Berkley.

Beasley, J. (2016). Repudiate the Doctrine of Discovery: An open letter to Pope Francis. Retrieved from: http://www.counterpunch. org/2016/10/03/repudiate-the-doctrine-of-discovery-an-open-letter-to-pope-francis/.

Benson, E. (2002). The synaptic self: Without synaptic plasticity, learning and the self, would be impossible. *Monitor on Psychology, November, Vol 33*, No. 10. American Psychological Association.

Berger S.L., Kouzarides T, Shiekhattar R, Shilatifard A (2009). An operational definition of epigenetics. *Genes & Development*, 23, (7): 781–3.

Berry, C. (2001). Andrew Jackson: The Worst President the Cherokee Ever Met. Retrieved from: www.allthingscherokee.com/andrew-jackson-worst-president-cherokee-ever-met/.

Berstein, A. (2016). Epigenetics, pregnancy and the Holocaust: How trauma can shape future generations. Retrieved from: https:// www.geneticliteracyproject.org/2016/08/21/epigenetics-pregnancy-holocaust-trauma-can-shape-future-generations.

Bielek, A. (2000). The Philadelphia experiment and Montauk survivor accounts. Retrieved from: http://www.bielek.com/.

Black, E. (2012). *War against the weak: Eugenics and America's campaign to create a master race.* Four Walls Eight Windows.

Black, K. (1996). *A healing homiletic: Preaching and disability.* Nashville: Abingdon Press.

Bowen, M. (1993). *Family therapy in clinical practice.* Jason Aronson, Inc.

Bowlby, J. (1982). *Loss: Sadness and depression, volume 3.* Basic Books Classics.

Bracha, S. (2004). Freeze, flight, fight, fright, faint: Adaptationist perspectives on the acute stress response spectrum. *CNS spectrums,* 9, (9): 679-85.

Bremner, J.D. (2006). Traumatic stress: effects on the brain. *Dialogues in clinical neuroscience,* 8, (4):445-61.

Bruinius, Harry. (2006). *Better for all the world: The secret history of forced sterilization and America's quest for racial purity.* A.A. Knopf.

Bryant, R.A. (2016). *Acute stress disorder: What it is and how to treat it.* Guilford Press.

Bullard, D. (2014). Interview with Bessel Van de Kolk: Trauma, development and healing. Retrieved from: www.psychotherapy.net/interview/bessel-van-der-kolk-trauma.

Byock, I. (2014). *The four things that matter most, 10th anniversary edition: A book about living.* Atria Books.

Carac, T. (2016). Urge Pope Francis to abandon the canonization of Junipero Serra. Retrieved from: http://petitions.moveon.org/sign/urge-pope-francis-to.

Carey, N. (2012). *The epigenetics revolution: How modern biology is rewriting our understanding of genetics, disease, and inheritance.* Columbia University Press.

Castillo, E. (2015): *A cross of thorns: The enslavement of California's Indians by the Spanish missions.* Craven Street Books.

Centre for Justice and Reconciliation (2017). Lesson 1: What is restorative justice? Retrieved from: http://restorativejustice.org/restorative-justice/about-restorative-justice/tutorial-intro-to-restorative-justice/lesson-1-what-is-restorative-justice/.

Chapman, A. and Van der Merwe, H., editors. (2008). *Truth and reconciliation in South Africa: Did the TRC deliver?* University of Pennsylvania Press.

Chen, M. (2007). *Western Shoshone struggle earns world recognition.* The New Standard.

Chenery, S. (2011). I can still hear the kids' screams. *The Sydney Morning Herald* (June 12).

Child Migrants Trust (2016). Child migration history. Retrieved from: http://www.childmigrantstrust.com/our-work/child-migration-history/.

Chrisjohn, R. D., Young, S.L., and Maraun, M. (1994). *The circle game: Shadows and substance in the Indian residential school experience in Canada. A report to the royal commission on aboriginal peoples.*

Cohen, J.A., Mannario, A.P., and Deblinger, E. (2017). *Treating trauma and traumatic grief in children and adolescents, second edition.* Guilford Press.

Coldey, B.M. (1995). *Child migration to catholic institutions in Australia.* Tamanaraik Publishing.

Coleman, William S.E. (2000). *Voices of wounded knee.* University of Nebraska Press.

Cooper, M. (1999). *Indian school: Teaching the white man's way.* Clarion Books.

Corless, A. (2014, November 3). Judging the past [Web log post]. Retrieved from https://kettleontherange.com/category/tuam-babies.

Coyle, S. (2014). Intergenerational trauma: Legacies of loss. *Social Work Today,* Vol. 14, No. 3.

Davis, J. (2016, March 3). Can trauma be passed on through our DNA? [Web log post]. Retrieved from http://upliftconnect.com/intergenerational-trauma.

Davenport, C. (1903). *Letter: Charles B. Davenport to John S. Billings.* Cold Spring Harbor beginnings correspondence a summary of progress.

Davenport, C. (1935). *Heredity in relations to genetics.* McMillian company.

Davenport, F. G. (1917). *European Treaties bearing on the history of the United States and its dependencies to 1648,* Vol. 1, Washington, D.C.: Carnegie Institution of Washington.

Deloria, V. (2003). *God is red: A native view of religion, 30th anniversary edition.* Fulcrum Publishing.

Dias, B., and Ressler, K. J. (2014). Parental olfactory experience influences behavior and neural structure in subsequent generations. *Nature Neuroscience, 17,* 89-96.

Dias, B. (2016). Phobias may be memories passed down in genes from ancestors. Retrieved from: http://www.telegraph.co.uk/news/science/science-news/10486479/Phobias-may-be-memories-passed-down-in-genes-from-ancestors.html.

Dilenschneider, A. (2013). *An invitation to restorative justice: The Canton asylum for insane Indians.* Northern Plains Ethics Journal.

Disability Rights Texas. (2010). History. Retrieved from: http://www.advocacyinc.org/who-we-are/history/.

Dodds, G. (2003). Political apologies: Chronological lists. Retrieved from: http://www.upenn.edu/pnc/politicalapologies.html.

Duffell, N. and Basset, T. (2016). *Trauma, abandonment and privilege: A guide to therapeutic work with boarding school survivors.* Routledge.

Erikson, E. (1994). *Identity and the Life Cycle* W. W. Norton & Company.

Erikson, K. T. (1976). *Everything in its path: Destruction of community in the Buffalo Creek flood.* Simon and Schuster.

Feldman, R. (2007). Parent–infant synchrony and the construction of shared timing: Physiological precursors, developmental outcomes, and risk conditions. *Journal of Child Psychology and Psychiatry, 48,* 329–354.

Ferentz, L. (2014). *Treating self-destructive behaviors in trauma survivors: A clinician's guide, second edition.* Routledge.

Final Call. (2008). Did Tuskegee damage trust on clinical trials? Retrieved from: http://www.finalcall.com/artman/publish/ NationalNews2/DidTuskegeedamagetrustonclinicaltrials4522. shtml.

Finn, C. (2014). Ten mother and baby homes carried out vaccine trials on almost 300 children. Retrieved from: http://www.thejournal. ie/baby-deaths-mother-baby-homes-1506811-Jun2014/.

Friedman, M.J. (2015). *Posttraumatic and acute stress disorders, sixth edition.* Springer.

Freud, S. (1917). *Mourning and melancholia.* Reprinted in: J. Strachey (trans. and ed.), Standard edition of complete psychological works of Sigmund Freud, Volume 14. London: Hogarth Press and Institute of Psychoanalysis (1957).

Galton, F. (1883). *Inquiries into human faculty and its development.* Macmillan; First American Edition.

Garcia, S. (2013). 8 Shocking Facts About Sterilization in U.S. History. Retrieved from: https://mic.com/articles/53723/8-shocking-facts-about-sterilization-in-u-s-history#.HauVdwQq0.

Garrigues, L.G. (2013). Slave and slave holders break free of history's trauma. *Yes Magazine,* August 2.

Geddes, L. (2013). *Fear of a smell can be passed down several generations.* New Scientist. Retrieved from: www.newscientist.com/ article/dn24677-fear-of-a-smell-can-be-passed-down-several-generations/.

Geiger, M. (1959). The life and times of Fray Junípero Serra: The man who never turned back. *Academy of American Franciscan History*, vol. 1.

Grant, M. (1936). *The passing of the great race*. Charles Scribner's Sons.

Grobecker, E. (2008), *Introduction as found in awaken to the immortal spirit*. Yug Purush Mahamandaleshwar Swami Paramanand Giriji Maharaj. Akhand Paramdham, Reg.

Hall, P. S. (1991). *To have this land: The nature of Indian/white relations: South Dakota: 1888-1891*. University of South Dakota Press.

Hamber, B. (1995). *Dealing with the past and the psychology of reconciliation*. Public address presented at the 4th International Symposium "Contributions of Psychology to Peace. Retrieved from: www.csvr.org/org/articles/artrcdrt.htm.

Hamber, B. (1996). The need for a survivor-centered approach to the truth and reconciliation commission. Munity Mediation update. Retrieved from: http://www.csvr.org.za/articles/artrcdrt.htm.

Hamber, B. & Wilson, R. (2002). Symbolic closure through memory, reparation and revenge in post-conflict societies. Research Papers. Paper 5. Retrieved from: http://digitalcommons.uconn.edu/hri_papers/5.

Haught, J.A. (2002). *Holy horrors: An illustrated history of religious murders and madness*. Prometheus.

HeartMath Institute (2008). The heart-brain synchronization between mother and baby. Retrieved from: https://www.heartmath.org/articles-of-the-heart/science-of-the-heart/mother-baby-study-supports-heart-brain-interactions/.

Helmenstine, A. (2015). DNA vs. RNA. Retrieved from: http://chemistry.about.com/od/lecturenoteslab1/a/Dna-Versus-Rna.htm.

Herman, J. (2015). *Trauma and recovery: The aftermath of violence—from domestic abuse to political terror.* Basic Books.

Hess, R., editor. (2015). *Mein kampf, my struggle: Unabridged edition of Hitler's original book – Four and a half years of struggle against lies, stupidity, and cowardice.* Haole Library.

Hopkins, R. (November 04, 2011. The Hiawatha asylum for insane Indians. Indian Country Today Media Network.

Houck, J. (2010). *Redeeming the bereaved: A spiritual model for healing our woundedness.* Xulon Press.

Houck, J. (2014). *Reclaiming authenticity: A psycho-spiritual process of transformation and transcendence.* WestBow Press.

Houska, T. (2015). California Ousts Native American Slur – Happy Indigenous Peoples Day, Indeed. Retrieved from: https://indiancountrymedianetwork.com/news/native-news/houska-california-ousts-native-american-slur-happy-indigenous-peoples-day-indeed/.

Hunt, D. (2012). BIA's Impact on Indian Education Is an Education in Bad Education. Retrieved from: https://indiancountrymedia network.com/news/bias-impact-on-indian-education-is-an-education-in-bad-education/.

Hurley, D. (2015). Grandma's experiences leave a mark on your genes. *Discover Magazine,* June 25.

Icke, D. (1999). *Heal the world: A do-it-yourself guide to human & planetary transformation.* Gill & MacMillan.

International Center for Transitional Justice. (2016). What is Transitional Justice? Retrieved from: www.ictj.org/about/transitional-justice.

Joinson, C. (2016). *Vanished in Hiawatha: The story of the Canton Asylum for insane Indians.* Bison Books.

Jones, J. (1981). *Bad blood: The Tuskegee syphilis experiment.* New York: Free Press.

Johnson, R.D. (1999). *Tiger patterns: A guide to the Vietnam's war tigerstripe combat fatigue patterns and uniforms.* Schiffer Military Aviation History. Schiffer Publishing, Ltd.

Johnson, R. S. (2014). Codependency and Codependent Relationships. Retrieved from http://www.BPDFamily.com.

Knödel, N. (1995). *The thanksgiving of women after childbirth, commonly called the churching of women.* University of Durham.

Kubler-Ross, E. (2017). *On death and dying: What the dying have to teach doctors, nurses, clergy, and their own families.* Scribner.

Kohut, H. (1971). *Analysis of the self, monograth # 4.* International Universities Press.

Krase, K. (2014). History of Forced Sterilization and Current U.S. Abuses. Retrieved from: http://www.ourbodiesourselves.org/health-info/forced-sterilization/.

Law Library. (2016). American Law and Legal Information: Notable Trials and Court Cases, 1637 to 1832, Johnson v. McIntosh:

Significance, the Doctrine of Discovery, Impact. Retrieved from: http://law.jrank.org/pages/25514/Johnson-v-McIntosh-Impact. html">Johnson v. McIntosh – Impact.

Lawrence, J. (2000). The Indian health service and the sterilization of Native American women. *American Indian Quarterly, Vol. 24,* No. 3, pp. 400-419.

Lee, B. (1975). *Tao of Jeet Kune Do.* Black Belt Communications.

Lemmens, J. (2013). Illegal Truth and Reconciliation Commission Event Vancouver (TRC Review). Retrieved from: https:// theangelscanseeyou.wordpress.com/2013/09/28/illegal- truth-and-reconciliation-commission-event-2013-vancouver-trc-review/.

Levine, P. and Kline, M. (2006). *Trauma through a child's eyes: Awakening the ordinary miracle of healing: Infancy through adolescence.* North Atlantic Books.

Lindemann, E. (1979). *Beyond grief: Studies in crisis intervention.* Jason Aronson, Inc.

Linden, S. (2017). *They called it shell shock: Combat stress in the first world war* (Wolverhampton Military Studies). Helion and Company.

Littlemoon, W. (2009). *They called me uncivilized: The memoir of an everyday Lakota man from Wounded Knee.* iUniverse.

Lombardo, P.A. (2010). *Three generations, no imbeciles: Eugenics, the Supreme Court, and Buck v. Bell.* Johns Hopkins University Press.

Lumey, L.H. and Van Poppel, F.W. (1994). The Dutch famine of 1944-45: Mortality and morbidity in past and present generations. *Journal of the Society for the Social History of Medicine,* 7(2): 229-46.

Maslow, A. (2014). *Toward a psychology of being.* Sublime Books.

Mauriac, F. (2017). *Vipers' tangle.* Cluny Media LLC.

McCraty, R. (2004). The energetic heart: Bioelectromagnetic communication within and between people. *Clinical applications of bioelectromagnetic medicine,* edited by P. J. Rosch and M. S. Markov. New York: Marcel Dekker, 541-562.

McDonald, H. (2013). Ireland finally admits state collusion in magdalene laundry system. Retrieved from: https://www.theguardian.com/world/2013/feb/05/ireland-magdalene-laundry-system-apology.

McEvers, K. (2015). Pope Francis Apologizes For 'Grave Sins' Against Native People Of America. Retrieved from: http://www.npr.org/2015/07/10/421826430/pope-francis-apologizes-for-grave-sins-against-native-people-of-america.

McGoldrick, M. and Gerson, R. (2008). *Genograms: Assessment and intervention, third edition.* W.W. Norton & Company.

McGregor, R. (1997). *Imagined Destinies. Aboriginal Australians and the Doomed Race Theory, 1900–1972,* Melbourne: MUP.

Mehl-Madrona, L. (2010). *Healing the mind through the power of story.* Bear and Company.

Meraji, S.M. (2015). *Savior or villain? The complicated story of Pope Francis' next saint.* Retrieved from: http://www.npr.org/sections/

codeswitch/2015/09/10/437598791/savior-or-villain-the-complicated-story-of-pope-francis-s-next-american-saint.

Miller, F. (1928). *Meriam report: The problem of Indian administration.* National Indian Law Library.

Minow, M. (1998). Between vengeance and forgiveness: Facing history after genocide and mass violence. Boston, MA: Beacon Press.

Moore, C. (2014). *The resilience breakthrough: 27 tools for turning adversity into action.* Greenleaf Book Group Press.

Moore, C. (2004). Buck v. Bell: The test case for Virginia's eugenical sterilization act. *Eugenics: Three generations, no imbeciles, Virginia, eugenics and Buck Vs. Bell.* Historical Collections at the Claude Moore Health Sciences Library. University of Virginia.

Mountjoy, E. (2010). Clymer No. 1 Mine Disaster, August 26, 1926, Clymer, Indiana Co. Retrieved from: http://www.patheoldminer. rootsweb.ancestry.com/indclymer2.html.

Narvaez, D. (December 17, 2014). [Web log post]. Retrieved from: www.psychologytoday.com/blog/moral-landscapes/201412/ why-kids-should-be-protected-toxic-stress.

National Archives of Australia. (2007). *Aboriginal Protection Act 1869 (Vic).* Documenting Democracy.

Nelson, B (1982). Why are earliest memories so elusive? Retrieved from: http://www.nytimes.com/1982/12/07/science/why-are -earliest-memories-so-fragmentary-and-elusive.html.

Neville, A.O. (1947). *Australia's coloured minority: Its place in the community.* Sydney: Currawong Publishing Co.

Newman, B.M. and Newman, P.R. (2011). *Development Through Life: A Psychosocial Approach 12th Edition*. Cengage Learning.

Nichols, P. and Moon, P. 1992. *The Montauk project: Experiments in time*. Sky Books.

Noll, M. A. (1992). *A history of Christianity in the United States and Canada*. William B. Eerdmans Publishing.

Nouwen, H. (1999). *The inner voice of love: A journey from anguish to freedom*. Image Books.

Ó Fátharta, C. (December 1, 2014). Glaxo's murky past: Vaccine trials on children worse than first thought. Retrieved from http://www.irishexaminer.com/ireland/special-investigation–vaccine-trials-on-children-worse-than-first-thought-300247.html#.VHxcm4C7QgQ.facebook.

Office of the Secretary, United States Department of Health, Education and Welfare. (1979). *The Belmont report: Protection of human subjects; notice of report for public comment*. Federal Register. 44 (76): 23191–7.

Pargament, K. (1997). *The psychology of religion and coping: Theory, research, and practice*. Guildford Press.

Pember, M.A. (2015). Trauma May Be Woven Into DNA of Native Americans. Retrieved from: http://indiancountrytodaymedianetwork.com/2015/05/28/trauma-may-be-woven-dna- native-americans-160508.

Pembrey, M. (2013). Phobias may be memories passed down in genes from ancestors. Retrieved from: http://www.telegraph.co.uk/news/science/science-news/10486479/

Phobias-may-be-memories-passed-down-in-genes-from-ancestors.html.

Perdue, T, (2003). *Both white and red. Mixed blood Indians: Racial construction in the early south.* The University of Georgia Press.

Petersen, A.C., Joseph, J., and Feit, M., editors. (2014). *New directions in child abuse and neglect research.* National Academies Press.

Peterson, C., & Seligman, M. E. P. (2004). *Character strengths and virtues: A handbook and classification.* New York: Oxford University Press and Washington, DC: American Psychological Association. www.viacharacter.org.

Philo, J. (2015). *Does my child have PTSD?: What to do when your child is hurting from the inside out.* Familius.

Pilkington, D. (2013). *Follow the rabbit-proof fence.* University of Queensland Press; Reprint edition.

Pollak, S. (2015). Magdalene survivor: They're ignoring my basic human rights. Retrieved from the link: http://www.irishtimes.com/news/social-affairs/magdalene-survivor-they-re-ignoring-my-basic-human-rights-1.2071627.

Powe, N. R., Sherber, N., Schulman, S. and Ding, E. (2008). Trust between doctors and patients is culprit in efforts to cross racial divide in medical research. Retrieved from:

http://www.hopkinsmedicine.org/heart_vascular_institute/media/press_releases/trust.html

Pratt, R. H. (2004). *Battlefield and classroom: Four decades with the American Indian.* University of Oklahoma Press.

Rael, J. (2015). *Being and vibration.* Council Oaks Books.

Rael, J. (2012). *Sound: Native teachings and visionary art of Joseph Rael.* Millchap Books.

Rheault, D. (2011). Solving the "Indian Problem" Assimilation Laws, Practices & Indian

Residential Schools. Retrieved from: http://www.omfrc.org/wp-content/uploads/2016/06/specialedition8.pdf.

Rinaldi, A. (1999). *My heart is on the ground: The diary of Nannie Little Rose, a Sioux girl, Carlisle Indian School, Pennsylvania 1880.* Scholastic Inc.

Roberts, J, (2008). *Massacres to mining: The colonization of aboriginal Australia.* Impact Investigative Media Productions.

Robertson, L.H. (2006). *The residential school experience: Syndrome or historic trauma.* Doctoral Candidate, Counselling Psychology: University of Calgary.

Rutecki, G.W. (2010). Forced Sterilization of Native Americans: Late Twentieth Century

Physician Cooperation with National Eugenic Policies. Retrieved from: https://cbhd.org/content/forced-sterilization-native-americans-late-twentieth-century-physician-cooperation-national.

Ryan, L. (2008). *A very bad business: Henry Dangar and the Myall Creek Massacre of 1838.* Retrieved from: http://www.academia.edu/8894929/AverybadbusinessHenryDangarandtheMyall Creek massacre 1838.

Samuels, D. (2014). Do Jews carry trauma in our genes? A conversation with Rachel Yehuda. Retrieved from: http://www.tabletmag.com/jewish-arts-and-culture/books/187555/trauma-genes-q-a-rachel-yehuda.

Sandwell, P. (2008). *Solving people's problems for the creation and preservation of family wealth*. Private Printing.

Schaverien, J. (2015). *Boarding school syndrome: The psychological trauma of the 'privileged' child*. Routledge.

Serra, J. (1955). *Writings of Junípero Serra*. Academy of American Franciscan History.

Seyle, H. (1974). *Stress without distress*. J. B. Lippincott Company.

Sherman, L.W. and Strang, H. (2007). *Restorative justice: The evidence*. The Smith Institute.

Siegel, D. (2015). Brain Insights and Well-Being. Retrieved from: http://www.drdansiegel.com/blog/2015/01/22/brain-insights-and-well-being-3/

Sims, J.M. (2010). A brief review of the Belmont Report. *Dimensions of Critical Care Nursing, July-August (4)*, 173-4.

Slomanson, W. (2011). *Fundamental Perspectives on International Law*. Boston, USA: Wadsworth. pp. 4–5.

SouthWings. (2016). Coal slurry and coal ash. Retrieved from: http://www.southwings.org/our-work/coal-slurry-ash/.

Spencer, H. (1995). *Social statistics: The conditions essential to human happiness specified, and the first of them developed*. Robert Schalkenbach Foundation.

Spencer, H. (1852). A Theory of Population, Deduced from the General Law of Human Fertility". *Westminster Review, 57*, 468–501.

Stein, D., Seedat, S., Kaminer, D., Moomal, H., & Herman, A. (2008). The impact of the truth and reconciliation commission on psychological distress and forgiveness in South Africa. *Social Psychiatry and Psychiatric Epidemiology, 43*(6), 462-468.

Stern, A. (2005). Sterilized in the name of public health: Race, immigration and reproductive control in modern California. *American Journal of Public Health, July, 95*(7): 1128–1138.

Stern, G.M. (2008). *The buffalo creek disaster: How the survivors of one of the worst disasters in coal-mining history brought suit against the coal company-and won.* Vintage.

Story, J. (1833). *Commentaries on the Constitution of the United States, volume 1.* Little, Brown & Co.

Swami Paramanand ji Maharaj. (2007). *Inner peace: A guide to venturing within.* Haridwar, India: Akhand Paramdham Reg.

Tedeschi, M. (2014). The Myall Creek massacre re-examined. *Inside History Magazine,* June 4.

Thacher, J. B. (1903). *Christopher Columbus, volume. 11.* G.P. Putman's Sons.

Thomson, H. (2015). Study of Holocaust survivors finds trauma passed on to children's genes. Retrieved from: https://www.theguardian.com/science/2015/aug/21/study-of-holocaust-survivors-finds-trauma-passed-on-to-childrens-genes.

Totten, C. (2009). The international criminal court and truth commissions: A framework for cross interaction in the Sudan and beyond. *Northwestern Journal of International Human Rights, Volume 7, Issue 1.*

Tronick, E., Adamson, L.B., Als, H., & Brazelton, T.B. (1975). *Infant emotions in normal and pertubated interactions.* Paper presented at the biennial meeting of the Society for Research in Child Development, Denver, CO.

United Nations. (2012). *Doctrine of Discovery: Used for Centuries to Justify Seizure of Indigenous Land.* Subjugate Peoples, Must Be Repudiated by United Nations, Permanent Forum Told. Retrieved from: http://www.un.org/press/en/2012/hr5088. doc.htm.

United States Environmental Protection Agency. (2016). Background on Drinking Water Standards in the Safe Drinking Water Act (SDWA). Retrieved from: https://www.epa.gov/dwstandardsregulations/background-drinking-water-standards-safe-drinking-water-act-sdwa.

Updegraff, J.A., Silvler, R.C., and Holman, E.A. (2008). Searching for and finding meaning in collective trauma. *Journal of Personal and Social Psychology,* September.

Van der Kolk, B. (2005). Developmental trauma disorder. *Psychiatric Annals, 35(5),* 401-408.

Van der Kolk, B. (2015). *The body keeps ther score: Brain, mind, and body in the healing of trauma.* Penguin Books; Reprint edition.

Vygotsky, L. S. (1978). *Mind in society: The development of higher psychological processes.* Cambridge: Harvard University Press.

Waddington C.H. (1942). The epigenotype. *Endeavour* 1:18–20. Reprinted in the *International Journal of Epidemiology, 2012, 41*:10–13.

Watada, T. (2006). *Obon: The festival of the dead.* Thistledown Press.

Weisel, E. (2006). *Night.* Hill and Wang.

Wenham, G.J. (1979). *The book of Leviticus.* Eerdmans.

Wong, E. (2013). A Shameful History: Eugenics in Virginia. Retrieved from: https://acluva.org/10898/a-shameful-history-eugenics-in-virginia/.

Wood, D., Bruner, J., & Ross, G. (1976). The role of tutoring in problem solving. *Journal of Child Psychology and Child Psychiatry, 17,* 89–100.

Woodard, S. (2011). South Dakota boarding school survivors detail sexual abuse. Retrieved from: http://indiancountrytoday medianetwork.com/2011/07/28/south-dakota-boarding-school-survivors-detail-sexual-abuse-42420.

Worden, J. W. (2018). *Grief counseling and grief therapy: A handbook for the mental health practitioner, fifth edition.* Springer Publishing Company.

Appendix A

The Doctrine of Discovery

The Bull Romanus Pontifex (Nicholas V), January 8, 1455.
Nicholas, bishop, servant of the servants of
God. for a perpetual remembrance.

The Roman pontiff, successor of the key-bearer of the heavenly kingdom and vicar of Jesus Christ, contemplating with a father's mind all the several climes of the world and the characteristics of all the nations dwelling in them and seeking and desiring the salvation of all, wholesomely ordains and disposes upon careful deliberation those things which he sees will be agreeable to the Divine Majesty and by which he may bring the sheep entrusted to him by God into the single divine fold, and may acquire for them the reward of eternal felicity, and obtain pardon for their souls. This we believe will more certainly come to pass, through the aid of the Lord, if we bestow suitable favors and special graces on those Catholic kings and princes, who, like athletes and intrepid champions of the Christian faith, as we know by the evidence of facts, not only restrain the savage excesses of the Saracens and of other infidels, enemies of the Christian name, but also for the defense and increase of the faith vanquish them and their kingdoms and habitations, though situated in the remotest parts unknown to us, and subject them to their own temporal dominion, sparing no labor and expense, in order that those kings and princes, relieved of all obstacles, may be the more animated to the prosecution of so salutary and laudable a work.

We have lately heard, not without great joy and gratification, how our beloved son, the noble personage Henry, infante of Portugal, uncle of our most dear son in Christ, the illustrious Alfonso, king of the kingdoms of Portugal and Algarve, treading in the footsteps of John, of famous memory, king of the said kingdoms, his father, and greatly inflamed with zeal for the salvation of souls and with fervor of faith, as a Catholic and true soldier of Christ, the Creator of all things, and a most active and courageous defender and intrepid champion of the faith in Him, has aspired from his early youth with his utmost might to cause the most glorious name of the said Creator to be published, extolled, and revered throughout the whole world, even in the most remote and undiscovered places, and also to bring into the bosom of his faith the perfidious enemies of him and of the life-giving Cross by which we have been redeemed, namely the Saracens and all other infidels whatsoever, [and how] after the city of Ceuta, situated in Africa, had been subdued by the said King John to his dominion, and after many wars had been waged, sometimes in person, by the said infante, although in the name of the said King John, against the enemies and infidels aforesaid, not without the greatest labors and expense, and with dangers and loss of life and property, and the slaughter of very many of their natural subjects, the said infante being neither enfeebled nor terrified by so many and great labors, dangers, and losses, but growing daily more and more zealous in prosecuting this his so laudable and pious purpose, has peopled with orthodox Christians certain solitary islands in the ocean sea, and has caused churches and other pious places to be there founded and built, in which divine service is celebrated. Also by the laudable endeavor and industry of the said infante, very many inhabitants or dwellers in divers islands situated in the said sea, coming to the knowledge of the true God, have received holy baptism, to the praise and glory of God, the salvation of the souls of many, the propagation also of the orthodox faith, and the increase of divine worship.

Moreover, since, some time ago, it had come to the knowledge of the said infante that never, or at least not within the memory of men, had it been customary to sail on this ocean sea toward the southern and eastern shores, and that it was so unknown to us westerners that we had no certain knowledge of the peoples of those parts, believing that he would best perform his duty to God in this matter, if by his effort and industry that sea might become navigable as far as to the Indians who are said to worship the name of Christ, and that thus he might be able to enter into relation with them, and to incite them to aid the Christians against the Saracens and other such enemies of the faith, and might also be able forthwith to subdue certain gentile or pagan peoples, living between, who are entirely free from infection by the sect of the most impious Mahomet, and to preach and cause to be preached to them the unknown but most sacred name of Christ, strengthened, however, always by the royal authority, he has not ceased for twenty-five years past to send almost yearly an army of the peoples of the said kingdoms with the greatest labor, danger, and expense, in very swift ships called caravels, to explore the sea and coast lands toward the south and the Antarctic pole. And so it came to pass that when a number of ships of this kind had explored and taken possession of very many harbors, islands, and seas, they at length came to the province of Guinea, and having taken possession of some islands and harbors and the sea adjacent to that province, sailing farther they came to the mouth of a certain great river commonly supposed to be the Nile, and war was waged for some years against the peoples of those parts in the name of the said King Alfonso and of the infante, and in it very many islands in that neighborhood were subdued and peacefully possessed, as they are still possessed together with the adjacent sea. Thence also many Guineamen and other negroes, taken by force, and some by barter of unprohibited articles, or by other lawful contract of purchase, have been sent to the said kingdoms. A large number of these have been converted to the Catholic faith, and it is hoped, by the help of divine mercy, that if such progress be continued with them, either those peoples will be converted to the faith or at least the souls of many of them will be gained for Christ.

But since, as we are informed, although the king and infante aforesaid (who with so many and so great dangers, labors, and expenses, and also with loss of so many natives of their said kingdoms, very many of whom have perished in those expeditions, depending only upon the aid of those natives, have caused those provinces to be explored and have acquired and possessed such harbors, islands, and seas, as aforesaid, as the true lords of them), fearing lest strangers induced by covetousness should sail to those parts, and desiring to usurp to themselves the perfection, fruit, and praise of this work, or at least to hinder it, should therefore, either for the sake of gain or through malice, carry or transmit iron, arms, wood used for construction, and other things and goods prohibited to be carried to infidels or should teach those infidels the art of navigation, whereby they would become more powerful and obstinate enemies to the king and infante, and the prosecution of this enterprise would either be hindered, or would perhaps entirely fail, not without great offense to God and great reproach to all Christianity, to prevent this and to conserve their right and possession, [the said king and infante] under certain most severe penalties then expressed, have prohibited and in general have ordained that none, unless with their sailors and ships and on payment of a certain tribute and with an express license previously obtained from the said king or infante, should presume to sail to the said provinces or to trade in their ports or to fish in the sea, [although the king and infante have taken this action, yet in time it might happen that persons of other kingdoms or nations, led by envy, malice, or covetousness, might presume, contrary to the prohibition aforesaid, without license and payment of such tribute, to go to the said provinces, and in the provinces, harbors, islands, and sea, so acquired, to sail, trade, and fish; and thereupon between King Alfonso and the infante, who would by no means suffer themselves to be so trifled with in these things, and the presumptuous persons aforesaid, very many hatreds, rancors, dissensions, wars, and scandals, to the highest offense of God and danger of souls, probably might and would ensue — We [therefore] weighing all and singular the premises with due meditation, and noting that since we had formerly by other letters of ours granted among other things free and ample faculty to the aforesaid King Alfonso — to invade, search out, capture, vanquish, and subdue all Saracens and pagans whatsoever, and other enemies of Christ wheresoever placed, and the kingdoms, dukedoms, principalities, dominions, possessions, and all movable and immovable goods whatsoever held and possessed by them and to reduce their persons to perpetual slavery, and to apply and appropriate to himself and his successors the kingdoms, dukedoms, counties, principalities, dominions, possessions, and goods, and to convert them to his and their use and profit — by having secured the said faculty, the said King Alfonso, or, by his authority, the aforesaid infante, justly and lawfully has acquired and possessed, and doth possess, these islands, lands, harbors, and seas, and they do of right belong and pertain to the said King Alfonso and his successors, nor without special license from King Alfonso and his successors themselves has any other even of the faithful of Christ been entitled hitherto, nor is he by any means now entitled lawfully to meddle therewith — in order that King Alfonso himself and his successors and the infante.may be able the more zealously to pursue and may pursue this most pious and noble work, and most worthy of perpetual remembrance (which, since the salvation of souls, increase of the faith, and overthrow of its enemies may be procured thereby, we regard as a work wherein the glory of God, and faith in Him, and His commonwealth, the Universal Church, are concerned) in proportion as they, having been relieved of all the greater obstacles, shall find themselves supported by us and by the Apostolic See with favors and graces — we, being very fully informed of all and singular the premises, do, motu proprio, not at the instance of King Alfonso or the infante, or on the petition of any other offered to us on their behalf in respect to this matter, and after mature deliberation, by apostolic authority, and from certain knowledge, in the fullness of apostolic power, by the tenor of these presents decree and declare that the aforesaid letters of faculty (the tenor whereof we wish to be considered as inserted word for word in these presents, with all and singular the clauses therein contained) are extended to Ceuta and to the aforesaid and all other acquisitions whatsoever, even those acquired before the date of the said letters of faculty, and to all those provinces, islands, harbors, and seas whatsoever, which hereafter, in the name of the said King Alfonso and of his successors and of the infante, in those parts and the adjoining, and in the more distant and remote parts, can be acquired from the hands of infidels or pagans, and that they are comprehended under *the said letters of faculty. And by force of those and of the present letters of faculty the acquisitions already made, and what hereafter shall happen to be acquired, after they shall have been acquired, we do by the tenor of these presents decree and declare have pertained, and forever of right do belong and pertain, to the aforesaid king and to his successors and to the infante, and that the right of conquest which in the course of these letters we declare to be extended from the capes of Bojador and of Não, as far as through all Guinea, and beyond toward that southern shore, has belonged and pertained, and forever of right belongs and pertains, to the said King Alfonso, his successors, and the infante, and not to any others. We also by the tenor of these presents decree and declare that King Alfonso and his successors and the infante aforesaid might and may, now and henceforth, freely and lawfully, in these [acquisitions] and concerning them make any prohibitions, statutes, and decrees whatsoever, even penal ones, and with imposition of any tribute, and dispose and ordain concerning them as concerning their own property and their other dominions. And in order to confer a more effectual right and assurance we do by these presents forever give, grant, and appropriate to the aforesaid King Alfonso and his successors, kings of the said kingdoms, and to the infante, the provinces, islands, harbors, places, and seas whatsoever, how many soever, and of what sort soever they shall be, that have already been acquired and that shall hereafter come to be acquired, and the right of conquest also from the capes of Bojador and of Não aforesaid.*

Moreover, since this is fitting in many ways for the perfecting of a work of this kind, we allow that the aforesaid King Alfonso and [his] successors and the infante, as also the persons to whom they, or any one of them, shall think that this work ought to be committed, may (according to the grant made to the said King John by Martin V., of happy memory, and another grant made also to King Edward of illustrious memory, king of the same kingdoms, father of the said King Alfonso, by Eugenius IV., of pious memory, Roman pontiffs, our predecessors) make purchases and sales of any things and goods and victuals whatsoever, as it shall seem fit, with any Saracens and infidels, in the said regions; and also may enter into any contracts, transact business, bargain, buy and negotiate, and carry any commodities whatsoever to the places of those Saracens and infidels, provided they be not iron instruments, wood to be used for construction, cordage, ships, or any kinds of armor, and may sell them to the said Saracens and infidels; and also may do, perform, or prosecute all other and singular things [mentioned] in the premises, and things suitable or necessary in relation to these; and that the same King Alfonso, his successors, and the infante, in the provinces, islands, and places already acquired, and to be acquired by him, may found and [cause to be] founded and built any churches, monasteries, or other pious places whatsoever; and also may send over to them any ecclesiastical persons whatsoever, as volunteers, both seculars, and regulars of any of the mendicant orders (with license, however, from their superiors), and that those persons may abide there as long as they shall live, and hear confessions of all who live in the said parts or who come thither, and after the confessions have been heard they may give due absolution in all cases, except those reserved to the aforesaid see, and enjoin salutary penance, and also administer the ecclesiastical sacraments freely and lawfully, and this we allow and grant to Alfonso himself, and his successors, the kings of Portugal, who shall come afterwards, and to the aforesaid infante. Moreover, we entreat in the Lord, and by the sprinkling of the blood of our Lord Jesus Christ, whom, as has been said, it concerneth, we exhort, and as they hope for the remission of their sins enjoin, and also by this perpetual edict of prohibition we more strictly inhibit, all and singular the faithful of Christ, ecclesiastics, seculars, and regulars of whatsoever orders, in whatsoever part of the world they live, and of whatsoever state, degree, order, condition, or pre-eminence they shall be, although endued with archiepiscopal, episcopal, imperial, royal, queenly, ducal, or any other greater ecclesiastical or worldly dignity, that they do not by any means presume to carry arms, iron, wood for construction, and other things prohibited by law from being in any way carried to the Saracens, to any of the provinces, islands, harbors, seas, and places whatsoever, acquired or possessed in the name of King Alfonso, or situated in this conquest or elsewhere, to the Saracens, infidels, or pagans; or even without special license from the said King Alfonso and his successors and the infante, to carry or cause to be carried merchandise and other things permitted by law, or to navigate or cause to be navigated those seas, or to fish in them, or to meddle with the provinces, islands, harbors, seas, and places, or any of them, or with this conquest, or to do anything by themselves or another or others, directly or indirectly, by deed or counsel, or to offer any obstruction whereby the aforesaid King Alfonso and his successors and the infante may be hindered from quietly enjoying their acquisitions and possessions, and prosecuting and carrying out this conquest.

And we decree that whosoever shall infringe these orders [shall incur the following penalties], besides the punishments pronounced by law against those who carry arms and other prohibited things to any of the Saracens, which we wish them to incur by so doing; if they be single persons, they shall incur the sentence of excommunication; if a community or corporation of a city, castle, village, or place, that city, castle, village, or place shall be thereby subject to the interdict; and we decree further that transgressors, collectively or individually, shall not be absolved from the sentence of excommunication, nor be able to obtain the relaxation of this interdict, by apostolic or any other authority, unless they shall first have made due satisfaction for their transgressions to Alfonso himself and his successors and to the infante, or shall have amicably agreed with them thereupon. By [these] apostolic writings we enjoin our venerable brothers, the archbishop of Lisbon, and the bishops of Silves and Ceuta, that they, or two or one of them, by himself, or another or others, as often as they or any of them shall be required on the part of the aforesaid King Alfonso and his successors and the infante or any one of them, on Sundays, and other festival days, in the churches, while a large multitude of people shall assemble there for divine worship, do declare and denounce by apostolic authority that those persons who have been proved to have incurred such sentences of excommunication and interdict, are excommunicated and interdicted, and have been and are involved in the other punishments aforesaid. And we decree that they shall also cause them to be denounced by others, and to be strictly avoided by all, till they shall have made satisfaction for or compromised their transgressions as aforesaid. Offenders are to be held in check by ecclesiastical censure, without regard to appeal, the apostolic constitutions and ordinances and all other things whatsoever to the contrary notwithstanding. But in order that the present letters, which have been issued by us of our certain knowledge and after mature deliberation thereupon, as is aforesaid, may not hereafter be impugned by anyone as fraudulent, secret, or void, we will, and by the authority, knowledge, and power aforementioned, we do likewise by these letters, decree and declare that the said letters and what is contained therein cannot in any wise be impugned, or the effect thereof hindered or obstructed, on account of any defect of fraudulency, secrecy, or nullity, not even from a defect of the ordinary or of any other authority, or from any other defect, but that they shall be valid forever and shall obtain full authority. And if anyone, by whatever authority, shall, wittingly or unwittingly, attempt anything inconsistent with these orders we decree that his act shall be null and void. Moreover, because it would be difficult to carry our present letters to all places whatsoever, we will, and by the said authority we decree by these letters, that faith shall be given as fully and permanently to copies of them, certified under the hand of a notary public and the seal of the episcopal or any superior ecclesiastical court, as if the said original letters were exhibited or shown; and we decree that within two months from the day when these present letters, or the paper or parchment containing the tenor of the same, shall be affixed to the doors of the church at Lisbon, the sentences of excommunication and the other sentences contained therein shall bind all and singular offenders as fully as if these present letters had been made known and presented to them in person and lawfully. Therefore let no one infringe or with rash boldness contravene this our declaration, constitution, gift, grant, appropriation, decree, supplication, exhortation, injunction, inhibition, mandate, and will. But if anyone should presume to do so, be it known to him that he will incur the wrath of Almighty God and of the blessed apostles Peter and Paul. Given at Rome, at Saint Peter's, on the eighth day of January, in the year of the incarnation of our Lord one thousand four hundred and fifty-four, and in the eighth year of our pontificate.

APPENDIX B

The Bull Inter Caetera (Alexander VI), May 4, 1493

Pope Alexander VI. Demarcation Bull Granting Spain Possession of Lands Discovered by Columbus Rome, May 4, 1493. Broadside, 1 sheet. Alexander, bishop, servant of the servants of God, to the illustrious sovereigns, our very dear son in Christ, Ferdinand, king, and our very dear daughter in Christ, Isabella, queen of Castile, Leon, Aragon, Sicily, and Granada, health and apostolic benediction. Among other works well pleasing to the Divine Majesty and cherished of our heart, this assuredly ranks highest, that in our times especially the Catholic faith and the Christian religion be exalted and be everywhere increased and spread, that the health of souls be cared for and that barbarous nations be overthrown and brought to the faith itself. Wherefore inas- much as by the favor of divine clemency, we, though of insufficient merits, have been called to this Holy See of Peter, recognizing that as true Catholic kings and princes, such as we have known you always to be, and as your illustrious deeds already known to almost the whole world declare, you not only eagerly desire but with every effort, zeal, and diligence, without regard to hardships, expenses, dangers, with the shedding even of your blood, are laboring to that end; recognizing also that you have long since dedicated to this purpose your whole soul and all your endeavors—as witnessed in these times with so much glory to the Divine Name in your recovery of the kingdom of Granada from the yoke of the Saracens—we therefore are rightly led, and hold it as our duty, to grant you even of our own accord and in your favor those things whereby with effort each day more hearty you may be enabled for the honor of God himself and the spread of the Christian rule to carry forward your holy and praiseworthy purpose so pleasing to immortal God. We have indeed learned that you, who for a long time had intended to seek out and discover certain islands and mainlands remote and unknown and not hitherto discovered by others, to the end that you might bring to the worship of our Redeemer and the profession of the Catholic faith their residents and inhabitants, having been up to the present time greatly engaged in the siege and recovery of the kingdom itself of Granada were unable to accomplish this holy and praiseworthy purpose; but the said kingdom having at length been regained, as was pleasing to the Lord, you, with the wish to fulfill your desire, chose our beloved son, Christopher Columbus, a man assuredly worthy and of the highest recommendations and fitted for so great an undertaking, whom you furnished with ships and men equipped for like designs, not without the greatest hardships, dangers, and expenses, to make diligent quest for these remote and unknown mainlands and islands through the sea, where hitherto no one had sailed; and they at length, with divine aid and with the utmost diligence sailing in the ocean sea, discovered certain very remote islands and even mainlands that hitherto had not been discovered by others; wherein dwell very many peoples living in peace, and, as reported, going unclothed, and not eating flesh. Moreover, as your aforesaid envoys are of opinion, these very peoples living in the said islands and countries believe in one God, the Creator in heaven, and seem sufficiently disposed to embrace the Catholic faith and be trained in good morals. And it is hoped that, were they instructed, the name of the Savior, our Lord Jesus Christ, would easily be introduced into the said countries and islands. Also, on one of the chief of these aforesaid islands the said Christopher has already caused to be put together and built a fortress fairly equipped, wherein he has stationed as garrison certain Christians, companions of his, who are to make search for other remote and unknown islands and mainlands. In the islands and countries already discovered are found gold, spices, and very many other precious things of divers kinds and qualities. Wherefore, as becomes Catholic kings and princes, after earnest consideration of all matters, especially of the rise and spread of the Catholic faith, as was the fashion of your ancestors, kings of renowned memory, you have purposed with the favor of divine clemency to bring under your sway the said mainlands and islands with their residents and inhabitants and to bring them to the Catholic faith. Hence, heartily commending in the Lord this your holy and praiseworthy purpose, and desirous that it be duly accomplished, and that the name of our Savior be carried into those regions, we exhort you very earnestly in the Lord and by your reception of holy baptism, whereby you are bound to our apostolic commands, and by the bowels of the mercy of our Lord Jesus Christ, enjoy strictly, that inasmuch as with eager zeal for the true faith you design to equip and despatch this expedition, you purpose also, as is your duty, to lead the peoples dwelling in those islands and countries to embrace the Christian religion; nor at any time let dangers or hardships deter you therefrom, with the stout hope and trust in your hearts that Almighty God will further your undertakings. And, in order that you may enter upon so great an undertaking with greater readiness and heartiness endowed with benefit of our apostolic favor, we, of our own accord, not at your instance nor the request of anyone else in your regard, but out of our own sole largess and certain knowledge and out of the fullness of our apostolic power, by the authority of Almighty God conferred upon us in blessed Peter and of the vicarship of Jesus Christ, which we hold on earth, do by tenor of these presents, should any of said islands have been found by your envoys and captains, give, grant, and assign to you and your heirs and successors, kings of Castile and Leon, forever, together with all their dominions, cities, camps, places, and villages, and all rights, jurisdictions, and appurtenances, all islands and mainlands found and to be found, discovered and to be discovered towards the west and south, by drawing and establishing a line from the Arctic pole, namely the north, to the Antarctic pole, namely the south, no matter whether the said mainlands and islands are found and to be found in the direction of India or towards any other quarter, the said line to be distant one hundred leagues towards the west and south from any of the islands commonly known as the Azores and Cape Verde. With this proviso however that none of the islands and mainlands, found and to be found, discovered and to be discovered, beyond that said line towards the west and south, be in the actual possession of any Christian king or prince up to the birthday of our Lord Jesus Christ just past from which the present year one thousand four hundred ninety-three begins. And we make, appoint, and depute you and your said heirs and successors lords of them with full and free power, authority, and jurisdiction of every kind; with this proviso however, that by this our gift, grant, and assignment no right acquired by any Christian prince, who may be in actual possesssion of said islands and mainlands prior to the said birthday of our Lord Jesus Christ, is hereby to be understood to be withdrawn or taking away. Moreover, we command you in virtue of holy obedience that, employing all due diligence in the premises, as you also promise—nor do we doubt your compliance therein in accordance with your loyalty and royal greatness of spirit—you should appoint to the aforesaid mainlands and islands worthy, Godfearing, learned, skilled, and experienced men, in order to instruct the aforesaid inhabitants and residents in the Catholic faith and train them in good morals...

Appendix C

United Nations Resolution 96

Convention on the Prevention and Punishment
of the Crime of Genocide

Approved and proposed for signature and ratification or accession
by 1948

Entry into force: 12 January 1951, in accordance with article XIII

The Contracting Parties,

Having considered the declaration made by the General Assembly
of the United Nations in its resolution 96 (I) dated 11 December 1946
that genocide is a crime under international law, contrary to the spirit
and aims of the United Nations and condemned by the civilized world,

Recognizing that at all periods of history genocide has inflicted
great losses on humanity, and

Being convinced that, in order to liberate mankind from such an
odious scourge, international co-operation is required,

Hereby agree as hereinafter provided :

Article I

The Contracting Parties confirm that genocide, whether
committed in time of peace or in time of war, is a crime under
international law which they undertake to prevent and to punish.

Article II

In the present Convention, genocide means any of the following acts committed with intent to destroy, in whole or in part, a national, ethnical, racial or religious group, as such:

(a) Killing members of the group;
(b) Causing serious bodily or mental harm to members of the group;
(c) Deliberately inflicting on the group conditions of life calculated to bring about its physical destruction in whole or in part;
(d) Imposing measures intended to prevent births within the group;
(e) Forcibly transferring children of the group to another group.

Article III

The following acts shall be punishable:

(a) Genocide;
(b) Conspiracy to commit genocide;
(c) Direct and public incitement to commit genocide;
(d) Attempt to commit genocide;
(e) Complicity in genocide.

Article IV

Persons committing genocide or any of the other acts enumerated in article III shall be punished, whether they are constitutionally responsible rulers, public officials or private individuals...

Printed in the United States
By Bookmasters